S0-FNR-250

On Freedom

On FREEDOM

∞ ∞ ∞ ∞ ∞

ESSAYS FROM THE FRANKFURT CONFERENCE

Edited by
John A. Howard

Foreword by
Robert A. Nisbet

Devin-Adair, Publishers
Greenwich, Connecticut

Copyright © 1984 by The Rockford Institute.

All rights reserved. No portion of this book may be reproduced or transmitted in any form or by any means, electronic or mechanical, including photocopy, recording, or any information storage and retrieval system, without the written permission of Devin-Adair, Publishers, 6 North Water Street, Greenwich, Connecticut 06830.

Manufactured in the United States of America.

Publisher: C. de la Belle Issue
Managing Director: Roger H. Lourie
Cover Design: Allison Lewis
Book Design: Henry Johnson
Typesetting: American Graphics Corporation

Library of Congress Cataloging in Publication Data

On freedom.

Contents: For your freedom and ours / by Leopold Tyrmand—Between Aristotle and anarchy / by Nikolaus Lobkowicz—Beyond empiricism / by Leszek Kolakowski — [etc.]
  1. Liberty—Congresses. 2. Civilization, Modern—Congresses. 3. Culture—Congresses. 4. Democracy—Congresses. 5. Conservatism—Congresses. I. Howard, John A. (John Addison), 1921–
HM271.052   1984   306   83-18932
ISBN 0-8159-5520-0

Contents

Acknowledgments vii
Foreword: Robert A. Nisbet ix

I. Towards a New Philosophy of Freedom
   1. For Your Freedom, and Ours
      Remarks by Leopold Tyrmand   3
   2. Between Aristotle and Anarchy:
      The Moral Challenge of Freedom
      by Nikolaus Lobkowicz   7
   3. Beyond Empiricism: The Need for a
      Metaphysical Foundation for Freedom
      by Leszek Kolakowski   27

II. Freedom and the Market
   4. Movement in the Market: Mobility and
      Economics in the Free Society
      by Paul Johnson   39
   5. The Profits of Freedom: Investing in
      the Defense of Business
      by Arthur Shenfield   59

III. The Cultural Substances of Freedom
   6. Reopening the Books on Ethics: The
      Role of Education in a Free Society
      by John A. Howard   79
   7. Feeling Unfree: Freedom and
      Fulfillment in Contemporary Culture
      by Ronald Berman   95

8. New Hymns for the Republic: The
   Religious Right and America's
   Moral Purpose
   by Richard John Neuhaus   112

IV. Freedom and Unfreedom
   9. Confronting "The Russian Question":
      The Ideological Journey of a Generation
      by Melvin J. Lasky   133

Onomastic Index   155
Topical Index   157

Acknowledgments

The essays in this volume were presented at a conference entitled "For Your Freedom, and Ours," held in the historic Hotel Frankfurter Hof, Frankfurt am Main, Federal Republic of Germany, November 18-20, 1982.

The Rockford Institute of Rockford, Illinois, sponsored the event. The National Strategy Information Center, based in New York City, served as co-sponsor. The conference participants were, for the most part, younger Europeans moving into positions of influence in academia, journalism, and government.

We wish to express appreciation to Allan C. Carlson and Richard A. Vaughan, both affiliated with The Rockford Institute, who served as managers of the conference, and to Bryce Christensen, also of the Institute, who assisted in the editing of the manuscripts.

Partial funding for the conference and the preparation of this book was provided by a generous grant from The J. Howard Pew Freedom Trust, Philadelphia.

John A. Howard
Editor

Foreword

Rarely has so lustrous a group of minds come together for the purpose of examining the idea of freedom in the modern world. What they have in common is their singular dedication to the freedom of the individual in society and their strength of inquiry into the sources and contexts of freedom. Differences are solely those of emphasis. Taking the essays in their entirety, it would be very difficult to find a more thoughtful and eloquent testament to the role of freedom in modern civilization.

Appropriately, the essays which begin the volume are philosophic in nature. Leopold Tyrmand stresses "freedom's bitter ambiguities" and also its "nonnegotiable preciousness." Nikolaus Lobkowicz points out that freedom, vital though it is to a creative society, is not the highest and most important of values: "If freedom were our highest value, a dungeon would be the only real evil." That is, freedom takes on its importance only in the company of the values of morality we cherish. Leszek Kolakowski reminds us that the mere empirical experience of freedom is insufficient. If freedom is to prevail, it will ultimately be through our knowledge of the *"essentia* of being human, and such an *essentia,* we ought to admit, may never be deduced from gathering data about human behavior."

Paul Johnson and Arthur Shenfield, in distinctive ways, stress the economic requirements of freedom of whatever kind. Johnson writes: "Both from the study of history and from observation of the contemporary world, it has become clear to me that the destruction of economic freedom leads inevitably to the destruction of political freedom." Arthur Shenfield pinpoints the business enterprise as the core of a free economy: "Business needs the free society and the free society needs business. . . . Business has the right and duty to oppose collectivism vigorously long before the omnipotent state is reached."

The cultural substance of freedom has not been overlooked. John Howard points out that the mainstay of any culture is its system of education. In our time of educational chaos we must remind ourselves over and over "that the process of formal schooling is the mechanism by which society assures that the common interests are protected, and this is done by training the young to understand their nation." Ronald Berman shows us how images popular among intellectuals have impinged upon a true culture: the images of alienation, hedonism, and narcissism. "Contemporary culture," he observes, "has encouraged us to believe that if we are not happy we are oppressed." Richard Neuhaus addresses himself to religion and culture: "The task today is to reestablish the linkages of Judeo-Christianity and the democratic experiment. . . . Unless the ideal of democratic freedom is conceptually revitalized, the energies of religious revival can be moved also into antidemocratic directions."

Finally, in arresting conclusion, Melvin Lasky provides us with an intellectual autobiography of the past halfcentury, bringing out the frequency with which Western intellectuals, in seeming disillusionment with their own values of freedom and democracy, have turned to the totalitarianisms of the left: "Perhaps we have come to this, at the end of one American's intellectual journey: we need to be reminded of the old aphorism: the trouble with man is twofold. . . . He cannot learn truths which are too complicated. He forgets truths which are too simple."

Foreword

I am proud to have participated in the conference that yielded us this rich harvest of ideas on the problem of freedom. This volume offers a veritable feast of philosophic insight, historical comprehension, and unswervable devotion to democratic freedom.

Robert A. Nisbet

I.

TOWARDS A NEW PHILOSOPHY OF FREEDOM

1.

For Your Freedom, and Ours

Remarks by Leopold Tyrmand

I am here to welcome you on behalf of The Rockford Institute in northern Illinois. I have been selected to this honor because I am a Pole by birth, a European by dint of the cultural juices and passions that nourished and shaped me, and an American by choice. Man arrives at his own sense of freedom through varied existential processes: one of my formative academies of this meaning was precisely in this town [Frankfurt on the Main], just a few blocks from here in the Park Hotel restaurant, where—in 1943—I waited tables. That condition could have been correctly called *Zwangsarbeit*, or forced labor, but today I would rather emphasize its cognitive consequences. It certainly helped to refine a surmise I had nursed even before the war: that, to rephrase Voltaire, the contemporary instinct for liberty makes one have two countries—his own and America.

In prewar Europe the simple vicissitudes of history enabled one to develop that instinct. From my life's perspective, I thus could respectfully add to Voltaire's dictum that *only* in America does freedom become a gratifying experience, a supreme luxury of our epoch, which alone is enough to determine its universality.

To fulfill all the unremarkable ironies of my *Bildungsroman*, we should have held this conference on the Wiesenhüttenstrasse, where the Park Hotel still stands. This, however, would be an act of shallow revanchism quite remote from my true feelings. The actual triumph of my condition is in the circumstance that the faith in America and its sense of freedom, which sustained so many throughout the war, seems as fresh and valid to me now as it did when it was sentimentally vested in Ernest Hemingway, Gary Cooper, or Walt Disney—some of my generation's naive symbolizations of a fascinating and perhaps better world. Between then and now, I have learned that a few centuries of tinkering with freedom has resulted in a social reality with a balanced ledger of good and bad, merciful and horrifying, noble and trivial. I can think of no other nation with a more deeply ingrained awareness both of freedom's bitter ambiguities and of its nonnegotiable preciousness.

Objectivity needs many words; lyricism is best served by brevity. I'm positive that this conference will produce some profound interpretations of liberty. Freedom, all its mobilizing power notwithstanding, is a notion laden with myriad implications and purports. The longer we live, the more we suspect how deviously it can be perverted, and the less we trust the certitudes for which, 40 years ago, we were so ready to risk our lives. Let me, therefore, focus on one illustration, motivated as I am by what Italians call *intelletto d'amore*. In 1942, during my first Polish underground briefing in Vilna, now Lithuania, the music that disguised the meeting as a dance blasted Fats

Waller's "Ain't Misbehavin'"; in Oslo, Norway, in 1941, my Hjemmetronten cell's anthem was "A tisket, a tasket. . ." Ella Fitzgerald shouted words that were pregnant with hope: ". . . and someone help me find my basket and make me happy again . . ." and the entire gathering cheered. Is there a lesson in it? Does jazz teach us something about freedom—one of the most complex of all the spiritual and social concepts with which Judeo-Christian civilization ever had to struggle? There were some among us, certainly, who pondered the Constitution and the American promise, or dream, but for most of us the collective improvisation of a Dixieland combo came to mean, if only subliminally, the perfect emblem of freedom and all the necessary energy to defend it. It was an image of liberty whose dynamics, at that time, seemed invincible, the ultimate representation of free utterance, the typification of a situation where anyone plays his own tune, providing he submits to a wise and superior arrangement. Jazz was to us a system of latitudes subject to a freely accepted discipline of integral bonds between an individual and a group. As such, it became perhaps the best metaphor for liberty that any culture has ever come up with. It conveyed a message that there *is* a central authority—usually with a trumpet in hand—to which one is responsible for holding the proper key and beat and who is entitled to a proper share of expression—and this is exactly what constitutes the principle from which a genuine order of freedom emerges. It became the quintessential allegory for the pluralism of opportunities, within which anyone who knows how to use an instrument and contribute to a common sound can make a statement about what he believes is beautiful and true.

In 1943, in a Frankfurt *Wirtschaft* on Neue Mainzer Strasse, I listened, at a clandestine jam session, to

Sidney Bechet's "Really the Blues." I sat next to a German of my own age, in uniform but on leave. "It's my record," he said proudly. "I was in a Panzer division in France. When we took a town, the others went after pâté and I looked for the music shops." I asked, "What does this music make you think of?" "Free people," he said. "Don't ask me why." It sounded a bit pompous, but I often thought of it later, when facing the Kremlin's rabid harangues against American cultural imperialism. During the last several decades of our alleged invasion of minds, young people all over the world burned American libraries while singing American songs of protest and sporting American folklore garb that had been invented by a Jewish-Californian tailor, who, a century ago, prescribed cosmopolitan fashion for contemporary Russian dissidents, Italian jet-setters, Palestinian guerrillas, and Colombian drug dealers alike. But American imperialism does not fill other countries' schoolbooks with portraits of our heroes, or force other nations' newspapers to lie. Anyone who does not wish to listen to our music is free not to do so without fear of our tanks and bombers. Therefore, if those who wish us ill want to call our stance imperialism, so be it—and thank God for it, because it means that, regardless of all our sins and flaws, we are still pure in heart.

Mr. Tyrmand, author of *Notebooks of a Dilettante, The Rosa Luxemburg Contraceptives Cooperative,* **and several widely translated Polish novels, is vice-president of The Rockford Institute and editor of** *Chronicles of Culture.*

2.

Between Aristotle and Anarchy: The Moral Challenge of Freedom

Nikolaus Lobkowicz

In beginning a consideration of those issues I deem to be critical in defining Western freedom, I remember a phrase which my teacher in philosophy, the famous specialist in the history both of formal logic and of Marxist-Leninist thought, Father Bochenski, occasionally used when the courses began. He himself had learned it from his own academic teacher, so that it has the ring of the wisdom of three generations of scholars. It runs as follows: "A young teacher teaches his pupils what he hardly knows himself; a mature teacher communicates what he has mastered. But when he has become old and wise, he tells his students what he feels they ought to know." Father Bochenski used to add that although he still did not feel old, he would like to act as if he already were wise, and to ask us to follow his example while still young.

What he did not add, at least not explicitly, was a statement to the effect that the older one gets the less sure one is about what one really does know. The scholar trying to be truly wise is confronted with the dilemma that, although he knows what his pupils ought to know, he is not sure that he knows it himself. Of course, he knows a lot of historical facts, and even more about what people thought about these facts in the past. Yet his knowledge is embedded in a broader context which seems to complicate whatever details he is familiar with, in particular if he has become aware of the fact that the long history of human thought, its struggle with truth, is by no means only an accumulation of insights true and wise. It is, on the contrary, a mass of claims, many of which do not fit together and some of which contradict each other. It is not difficult to discover how each of them came about, but infinitely more difficult to say which of them is true and to what extent. The German philosopher Hegel once wrote that only the totality is true: "Die Wahrheit ist das Ganze." What he meant by this was that in order to fathom the truth of a single claim, we have to have penetrated that of all others. He ought to have added, and one of the many defaults of his lofty philosophical system was that he did not add it, that this claim applies to itself as well. To maintain that only the totality of all possible knowledge is truth is one claim among many others; it is a partial truth to the extent that we never could have any true insight at all if we did not have the courage to put forward claims true only to some extent.

Bearing this in mind, I would like to share a few reflections concerning freedom, equality and contemporary democracy. One of my aims is to suggest to you that much of the confusion of our age, and both the apathy and the passion issuing from it, is due to the immense complexity of truth, which, in turn, we owe to the fact that the history of human thought and of human concerns is very long. Whenever we try to articulate any principle or value according to which we orient our daily life, we discover that it is contradicted, or at least limited, by other values.

Take the basic dilemma of Christian life. Christians believe that the ultimate meaning of all our doings, of our lives as well as of the universe as a whole, does not rest with us alone. Yet few of us have the vocation to consequently withdraw into a monk's cell in order to contemplate what according to the Gospel is the one and only necessary concern. We lead lives which force us, as Jesus says to Martha, to "trouble about many things"; thereby, we risk losing sight of the "only real thing" (Luke 10:41-42). But if we did not have the courage to act, human society and what we call our world would crumble. Christian wisdom consists, among other things, in the composure that enables us to consider, and to do, things we know are not what really count. It consists in bearing and enduring, patiently and thoughtfully, the complexity of the human condition, which is never simple enough to permit us to master it by simple solutions.

Let me therefore say first that freedom is neither the highest nor the most important of human values. If it were, if your freedom and mine were the most important thing in our lives, we should be expected to risk everything for it, not only our well-being and our lives but also truth, morality, any order of any kind. Many were scandalized when former Secretary of State Haig said that there are more important things than peace; but he obviously was right, since anyone who declares peace the ultimate value is committed to give in, indeed to accept slavery, whenever peace is seriously threatened. Something of this kind applies to freedom as well. If freedom were our highest value, a dungeon would be the only real evil. And yet we admire people who accepted imprisonment "for a higher cause." You may object that many have gone to dungeons to save the freedoms of others. Yet, although this is true, it is also true that many have suffered bondage and serfdom for other causes, above all for their convictions and their moral integrity. This is one of the reasons why our Occidental culture, beginning with Plato and Aristotle, developed an ethics according to which man's goodness and, thereby, "happiness" is largely independent of circumstances which we cannot change. Holiness and, indeed, simple human goodness can be achieved everywhere, a dungeon not excluded. As a matter of fact, many observations suggest that people living in slavery, as under the contemporary communist systems, quite often develop more heroism and virtue than we who proudly speak of a Free West.

By this, of course, I do not mean to say that freedom is not a value worth fighting for. After all, it is the ideal of freedom that has brought about modern democracy, which for the time being all honest men consider the best political system ever found. Yet we should not overlook what else has happened in the name of freedom. We may forget that even today some modern states celebrate the anniversary of the murder of their ruler as a national holiday, but we cannot overlook the fact that we live in an age in which other aspects of our cultural and ethical heritage are daily cast off in the name of freedom. Some might even want to argue that there is a sort of logic in the development from a rebellion against rulers to the rebellion we everywhere witness today, against moral principles, against the most elementary experiences of mankind, indeed against man's nature itself. Neo-Marxists have described this logic in terms of the notion of an alienation to be overcome: by overthrowing rulers the nations reappropriate what was rightfully theirs, their sovereignty; by emancipating ourselves from legal or ethical norms we reappropriate our inner independence; by rebelling against everything that restrains us in any way, we find our way back from alienation to our genuine free self.

There have been many attempts to redefine freedom in such a way as to prevent conceptual abuses of this kind. Some tell us that true freedom is not freedom from something but rather to do something. Or we are told that genuine freedom consists of recognizing inevitable constraints. Some even would want to make us believe that freedom ultimately consists in recognizing the inevitable. Yet, whatever the merits of such claims, the primary meaning of freedom always will be the freedom from fetters. And this freedom, as important as it may be and as forcefully as we may have to defend it, is not all. The escaped criminal who immediately commits a new crime was free; but who would want to deny that he did not use his freedom the proper way?

It was the greatest error of liberalism to believe that the only problem of political philosophy consists in finding and maintaining a political system in which freedom of the individual is limited by nothing except the freedom of others. Such a system induces one to forget what older political philosophers maintained, namely that the ultimate end of all political order consists in helping man to be virtuous. After all, the liberal doctrine leads to a situation in which I may do whatever comes to my mind as long as I do not encroach upon others' chances to do the same. Such an outlook also ignores the fact that for others freedom might amount to no more than the freedom to starve, to the freedom of remaining an animal. It is this insight which since the fifth century B.C., when the notion of democracy began to take shape, induced thinkers to claim that freedom, even in its most abstract sense, has something to do with equality. When Athenian statesmen such as Pericles and later thinkers such as Aristotle tried to describe democracy as the political system of men free from all bondage, they noticed that, at least in some sense and to some extent, the citizens of this community have to be equal.

Originally, this equality meant nothing but being equal before the law. Whether of aristocratic or of peasant origin, whether poor or wealthy, each citizen of Athens had the same right to participate in decisions about how the constitution ought to be construed; and, in particular, whenever his case came before the court, he had the right to be judged without regard for such differences, at least as long as they did not issue from a special status. It is interesting to notice that the many ancient critics of democracy after the defeat of Athens in the Peloponnesian War mention the excesses both of freedom and of equality as its main defaults. Thus Plato, for example, accuses the citizens of democracies of dwelling in licentiousness and of distributing everything equally among equals and nonequals, which according to him is nothing but the expression of an undue forbearance (*Politeia*, 557b, 558c). And if you pursue the fate of the notion of democracy throughout the ages, it will always be equality together with freedom which will be mentioned as its gravest problems.

These problems concern us even today, which is why I want to explore them further. Plato, Aristotle, the Stoics and later the Christians fashioned the simple notion of freedom from fetters into a more complex concept of individual freedom. It was not until almost two thousand years later that the notion of the rule of the people became a prominent concern again. For this tradition, the goodness of men and the right order among them, not freedom, was the supreme human value. This is why they did not see freedom's fetters primarily in the bondage imposed upon men by men, but in the natural serfdom of man's higher to his lower abilities. According to this long tradition, real freedom consists in the rule of man's rational part over the irrational—of reason over passion, of man's divine capacities over his animal instincts. When the representatives of this tradition were suspicious of democracy, the reason was that they saw that on the one hand the individual himself was the main source of his own serfdom and that on the other hand the quest for equality inevitably induces men to agree on their lowest common denominator, upon man's animal features. This is why they felt that men ought to be ruled by the best, and that the best, not the common man, ought to be the standard against which the right order is to be measured. To them, democracy seemed to entail the danger that the lower aspects of the human condition would take over: passion over reason, the animal over the spirit, the uneducated mob over those who have succeeded in mastering man's animal parts. Their thought was aristocratic, not only in the original sense in which "aristocracy" means the rule of the *aristoi*, the best, but also in the modern sense that the crowd of mediocre was to be ruled according to the standards of the few whose personal effort, and later education, and still later origin, guaranteed the victory of the valuable over the mediocre or even the valueless.

Now, I do not want to lecture on the history of

the notions of freedom, equality, and democracy. Let me therefore restrict myself to saying that the modern result of this agelong discussion about the merits of freedom and liberty, of equality and of the superiority of the best, of popular democracy and of a republic ruled by the most worthy, is an ambiguity surrounding the notion of democracy. There are at least three different notions of democracy, all of which have become essential elements of our understanding of this institution. And although they are interconnected, they entail quite different claims concerning the relationship between freedom and equality. What we really mean by democracy almost entirely depends upon which of these three traditions we emphasize.

The first notion of democracy also has the longest tradition; I would call it the properly *political* notion of democracy. It construes democracy as a political system in which free men, equal before the law, decide by elections who will rule them. It is basically the notion of a republic, yet differs from it in two important respects: it takes equality seriously by not excluding from it any adult, neither because of race, nor because of sex, nor because of income, nor because of any other feature with the possible exception of unworthiness because of a crime. Secondly, it considers eligible for office anyone entitled to vote, with possible exceptions due to age requirements. Predemocratic republics did not fulfill either of these two conditions. In Athens, only the head of the family was entitled to vote; women and slaves were not even considered citizens. In the Republic of Venice, everyone was—although in a complicated way—entitled to participate in elections; but it was agreed that only the members of some families could become doge.

Emerging in America as early as 1647 when in the colonial records of Rhode Island the "forme of

Government in Providence Plantations" is called "Democraticall" and defined as "a Government held by ye free and voluntarie consent of all," this political notion of democracy implies an important semantic feature. It does not permit one to speak of anything such as a "democratization." Considered as a constitution or a political system, democracy in this sense may be more or less well constructed, but it can be more or less democratic no more than a racing horse is not more of a horse than a farm horse.

The notion of "democratization," of introducing more of democracy into a political system already democratic, presupposes a quite different idea. We discover it first in France during the decades preceding the Revolution of 1789. This second notion of democracy, which I would dub *social*, connotes a process rather than a system and centers around the notion of equality, not around that of freedom. It presupposes a situation in which some classes or groups, although they may be legally free and equal, are underprivileged. For them, or their protagonists, "democracy" is the battle cry in their fight for equality, for equal privileges and chances. Usually, this battle cry will be construed as one for freedom; this is the reason why this fight usually is described as an "emancipation," a term which originally meant the legal act by which a child became independent of his father. But it is important to see that this call for freedom differs from that which we hear when people fight for a political democracy. For those fighting for democracy in this case usually already are equals in the sense of what the Greeks called *isonomia*, equality before the law. What they fight for is not freedom, but the chance to use it more effectively. When the French bourgeoisie prior to the Revolution or when workers in the second half of the 19th century fought for democracy or when contemporary groups which either are or are believed to be underprivileged speak of a need for "more democracy," they already are free and equal in the formal political sense. They can participate in elections and theoretically even have an equal chance to be elected. But they are not really interested in who rules them; they are concerned about their chance to use their freedom in a way equal to that of those whom they describe as "the ruling class," or "the establishment," or "the privileged minority."

Let me add that although the political and the social meaning of the term *democracy* significantly differ, there is something like a historical logic in the development from a purely political democracy to a social democracy. In most instances, nations initially agree on a "government held by the free and voluntary consent of all" in a situation permitting a few who are wealthy and educated to do just what their hearts desire, while leaving many without wealth, without an access to education, and quite limited in their chances to use their freedom meaningfully. As the latter are the majority, they will strive for a government primarily serving their cause; and eventually they will get it. What will emerge is a situation exactly opposed to the aristocratic idea inherent in the traditional ethical concept of the right political order: those most ready to give in to what the majority desires, not the best, will be at the top, will be the rulers, will form the government.

However, before I dwell on the relationship between the political and the social dimension of democracy, let me add a word on a third notion. It is rarely consciously noticed and usually mentioned only when people qualify a behavior as democratic or undemocratic. I therefore call it either the *procedural* or the *behavioral* notion of democracy. When in a meeting of a school board, for example, the representatives of a minority are overruled and then declare that they will not accept the decision, they will be accused of not being democrats. Similarly, in the discussion that preceded the ruling, the speaker of the minority might appeal to the majority that it would be fair and democratic to give in at least in part to the motion of the minority. Or, to mention a recent German example, a political party might win adherents by claiming that they will enter a coalition with another party, and then will act otherwise. When their behavior is described as undemocratic, one thinks neither of the explicit rules of a political system nor of a development toward more equality but rather of some norms of human behavior. This third notion of democracy has a very strong moral connotation; it is something like the quintessence of the behavioral, moral norms of those who live under a democratic system.

Now, what we have witnessed during the last fifteen or twenty years is a powerful advance of the second, the special notion of democracy. The reasons for this development are manifold. One might mention the Catholic Church's accommodation to the modern world in the aftermath of Vatican II as well as to the tremendous impact which various shades of Western neo-Marxism have had on our culture. Also, one might invoke the new insistence on human rights or the new widespread concern for social issues. Last but not least one might puzzle over whether at least parts of this development are not the expression of the historical logic already outlined.

I am interested less in the causes than in the consequences of this development, and I would like to put forward the claim that it has significantly weakened our concern for freedom. For it is not the idea of social but that of political democracy which insists on freedom; the idea of social democracy, which one also might call welfare democracy, insists on equality. That the insistence on equality leads to a reduction in the concern for freedom is a very old insight; de Tocqueville insisted on it after his study of the United States in the 1830s. One might object that as a member of the French aristocracy, who was as sickened by what he observed as he was fascinated, he thought of freedom in aristocratic terms. He shrewdly observed that the privileged life would disappear as democracy spreads. For this reason many today claim that increasing equality ultimately increases equality of freedom, since the number of those enabled to share in freedom's fruits gets bigger.

There is certainly something to this argument. If freedom is a right of which one cannot avail oneself, it is little more than a word: if someone tells me that I am free to go wherever I wish but I am too weak to walk at all, my dismissal into freedom is nothing but a dirty trick. But to admit this must not make us blind to the fact that there are several interconnected ways in which mandated equality entails a curbing of freedom. To begin with, one may express some doubt as to whether an increase in the number of those who may be called socially free really can be characterized as a general "increase in freedom." Although the presuppositions of freedom certainly are social, the state of being free is something strictly individual. Literally speaking, it is never a society which is free but rather the members of some kinds of society. There is a very real sense in which to speak of an increase of freedom for all only because of an increase of the number of those who share in it is as preposterous as to claim, for example, that my pain is enhanced by many others suffering the same pain.

More important than this semantic point, however, is the fact that in modern society movement towards equality in most cases can be accomplished only by the state, and the state cannot give to anyone anything which it did not take away from someone else. To the extent that freedom, in order to be real, presupposes material means, any redistribution of these means amounts to a reduction of the presupposition of someone else's freedom. If only a few own landed property, it is only a few who can enjoy the kind of freedom that private ownership of landed property guarantees. If I redistribute this landed property, I certainly achieve greater equality, and thereby increase the number of those who can enjoy freedom ensuing from it, but I reduce the freedom of the original owners. When the state taxes a higher income at a higher rate than a low income, it leaves more freedom to persons with the latter but reduces the freedom of persons with the former.

One might reply, as many do, that while this may be the case, it is just. The underlying argument, in this case, is that it is unjust if some can and others cannot enjoy their freedom. But even if this were true (and it is true only to a limited extent), it nevertheless remains true that in the economic realm, equality is achieved at the expense of someone's freedom. Something of this kind seems to apply also to noneconomic fields. In recent decades we have all witnessed a rise in university education that has decreased both the average quality of that schooling and the professional prospects of university graduates. Even such a simple thing as stylish clothing loses its distinctive value, its privileged character, and its expressive freedom if everyone begins to wear it.

Another reason why increased equality entails a reduction of freedom of at least some is the fact that the redistribution of wealth, as we witness it in all Western democracies today, requires an ever-growing bureaucratic apparatus producing an ever-growing number of regulations. In this respect, in fact, it is everyone who suffers from the increasing equality of well-being. While modern democracies were established, among other reasons, under the pretext that they would reduce the load put on men by the state, we have a larger state today than any society of the past. Ours is a benevolent state, it is true, but, as everyone knows, even the greatest benevolence can become oppressive when it is connected with too many requirements.

I am neither an enemy of equality nor a passionate opponent of the welfare state. But it seems to me important to see that the advance of the social notion of democracy has its price. Even our wealthy societies seem not wealthy enough to expand their welfare system further. And, apart from that, the price we pay for the system is freedom. It may be inevitable and even just to have to pay it; but we should not forget that we do pay it—some of us more than others, but everyone to some extent.

There is another aspect of this question that is seldom noticed. To be free both entails and presupposes the risk of failure. That God gave me a free will entails the risk that I disavow Him. That I am a free owner of an enterprise entails the risk that I will wreck it. That I am member of a community of free men entails the risk that none of us will do justice to the other and that the community will fall apart. Now, one of the aims of our welfare democracies is to give everyone a security insulating failure from consequences. If I am too lazy to work seriously, I will receive public assistance. If I do not take care of my health, the state hospitals will cure me. If I do not save money for my old age, I will receive a pension. And if I want to swim on a California beach, mounted police will drive me away because of the sharks around; they will not simply warn me, but drive me away—as if I had no right to take a risk.

This development is a protuberance, as it were, of the social notion of democracy. If full equality is to be achieved, the state has to take care that nobody falls out of line. It has to guarantee everyone's security, and this not only in the classical sense in which the first duty of the state was to protect the life of its citizens but also in the paralyzing sense that the state has to take care of me every time I risk doing something that may harm myself in any way. The state cares for me whether I achieve something or not, whether I care for it or not.

This development curbs freedom in a way different from those mentioned before; it undermines my determination to make use of my freedom. In fact, it undermines my conviction that freedom is valuable. The consequence is a growing number of citizens who prefer both equality and security to freedom. Equality gives them a chance to be better off and security takes away from them all risk. What is freedom worth, an increasing number of citizens think, if it entails risks—the risk to fail, the risk of having to defend oneself, the risk of being forced to be responsible for what one does?

Originally, equality meant nothing but the equality of free men before the law; in the scales of the constitution, of the laws, of the courts, everyone ought to have the same chance. Since the end of the 18th century Western society has realized that this is too empty a notion of freedom. Freedom, in order to be real, implies *material* presuppositions. Hence the development of a social, as well as a political notion of democracy. Yet as time went on, there emerged a democracy reminding one of Hobbes's *Leviathan*: a state guaranteeing everyone's freedom and thereby increasingly curbing it. One of the reasons why the understanding of and commitment to the values of freedom and liberty rapidly has declined in our societies is the development of modern free societies themselves and indeed of the idea of freedom. Those defending the convergence theory, the claim that the Free Western World and communist countries will become indistinguishable in the long run, may be wrong as far as the liberalization of the communist system is concerned. They are not far from the truth concerning the "socialization" which is tacitly and surreptitiously making the West similar to the East.

Now the question is what we can do in the face of this threat. We may, of course, call for reasonable limits to the modern welfare state. It will not help much, though, since too many people—the recipients of the gifts as well as those administering them—are interested in its continuation and growth. To some extent they are even right in being interested in it. The modern welfare state is on the way to abolishing poverty, analphabetism, and inhuman conditions. The obvious danger that it might tumble will quite probably be averted for economic reasons alone. Welfare payments for all have become too costly to be financed even by a redistribution of wealth; ransacking the estates of all the wealthy people around would not permit a larger welfare system nor even maintain present programs. Apart from everything else, modern economics has shown that expropriation through taxes and other measures has its limits beyond which it is strictly counterproductive. You cannot successfully roast a steak from a cow which you want to continue to milk.

How, then, can we strengthen the understanding of and the commitment to freedom in our societies? To begin with, I do not think that it would be effective simply to extol freedom and liberty. On the other hand, the tide which we oppose is too powerful to be resisted by repeating words with which everyone is familiar. After all, for over 30 years the Free West has reverberated with praises of liberty, and still many, above all the young, do not seem to think highly of it. On the other hand, the freedom which we praise so much has become a problem for our age; too many do not know what to make of it. The Western world went through this experience once already, between the two World Wars: many were fascinated by the Soviet Union in the '20s and '30s. To them, the freedom which they daily experienced in the United States, in England, or on the European continent meant little compared to the thrust of the powerful ideas of the Marxists and, for that matter, of the Nazis. Above all intellectuals (who, because it is their task to reflect, are easily uprooted and alienated from everything that smacks of tradition) were fascinated by the novelty, indeed the ruthlessness of these ideologies.

Just as unprofitable as praising Western liberty is the cautionary attempt to point out what goes on in Eastern Europe or many countries of East Asia or in Cuba. Only because of human blindness was the impact of Solzhenitsyn's *Gulag* so tremendous. With a few exceptions, this book did not contain any information with which those who cared to be acquainted with what went on in the Soviet Union were not familiar. Whole libraries had been written on the subject, and nevertheless there were many, too many, who needed an admittedly powerful writer to convince them. As a German saying states, everything has its natural limits, except man's stupidity.

Let me also point out that many of our young do not know what to do with their freedom. They stumble from experiment to experiment: from drugs to intoxicating music, from secular messages of salvation to the most awkward religious sects, from quasi-marital unions to excitements about what happens in faraway countries. Some get caught in one or another of these experiments; others sober down and are disillusioned; still others lose the ability to commit themselves to anything whatsoever, including the freedom to experiment. The number of those who go through these experiences unscathed probably is much smaller than we care to believe.

It seems to me, therefore, that it is the *contents of freedom* on which we must concentrate, the human values which presuppose freedom and in turn enhance it. We have to try to get away from the idea that the ultimate meaning of freedom is to be able to do just what one likes, and possibly what the most base instincts suggest. In other words, while defending liberty and our political system which best guarantees it, we have to recover for our daily lives at least parts of the aristocratic tradition which underlies the ethics of the Occidental world. What would liberty be good for if we did not achieve the mastery over ourselves which alone permits us at least to try to be good men? Perhaps the Greeks and the Christians of the Middle Ages and early modern times oversimplified the matter when they claimed that once the higher abilities of man have mastered the lower ones, man becomes automatically good. They thought too much in terms of a divine element imprisoned in an animal and therefore believed that as soon as the former has mastered the latter it will turn to the Good like an eagle returns to his nest high in the mountains. But they certainly were right in one respect: in order to make the world more worth living in, in order to find the right uses of freedom, man first has to make the painful effort of turning himself against himself. To use an example mentioned by C. S. Lewis, man in his natural state is like a dog let free in the wilderness, dirty, undisciplined, and hardly lovable. Only when he is trained by his master, when he has overcome his untamed nature and developed his hidden soul, does he become the dog which is our friend. Lewis uses this example in order to characterize God's use of pain to educate us to be His servants. But it also would seem to apply to the way in which we humans ought to educate both ourselves and our children. Freedom is an instrument which can be used for good as well as for evil. Our task is to train ourselves and others to use it for that which the Occidental tradition has called virtue, for man's being a good man, a man with a fully developed human nature. This may sound abstract. But the simple practical message which I would draw from it is that man's freedom has a natural end other than arbitrariness; that the end to which man uses his freedom is not a matter of indifference; and that man cannot appreciate his freedom until he has accepted a self-imposed bondage, the bondage of the little good in himself over the mass of animal desires, irrationality, fanaticism, and lack of patience and composure which tug him about. Our young, the generation we all set our hopes in, will not be convinced about the value of freedom until and unless we again teach them that to be free and to use one's freedom meaningfully entails an effort that inevitably is painful.

This message may sound hopeless. For how should we, in a world as mentally chaotic as ours, save our liberty if it presupposes a moral change in our innumerable fellow citizens? How shall we ever succeed if the fate of democracy depends upon such a simple thing as the personal morality of each and every individual man? How should we create a new awareness of American and European freedom if everything depends upon a moral renewal?

I have no ready answer to this question. But I want to mention an answer which Aristotle suggests on the last pages of his *Nicomachean Ethics*. After having completed this monumental work, the first thoroughly thought-out ethical system of the Occident, he discusses the question as to whether morality really can be furthered by laws and rules. He arrives at the conclusion that it usually does not work out. But then he adds that perhaps it may be enough if a free man succeeds in teaching his children and friends and servants what striving for goodness means. It is the same with freedom. One can lecture about it, organize conferences around it, preach it, but the only real way to carry it on, to maintain, to save it, is through our personal example, through the conduct of our own lives in the circle of the few with whom we are personally acquainted.

Dr. Lobkowicz, author of *Historical Laws: Studies in Soviet Thought* and several other studies of the Soviet Union and the West, is professor of political theory and philosophy at the University of Munich.

3.

Beyond Empiricism: The Need for a Metaphysical Foundation for Freedom

Leszek Kolakowski

Who is against freedom? The answer is simple: nobody, absolutely nobody. In all wars "freedom" is invariably on both sides. All the varieties of genocide, terror, persecution, of whatever hue, are being committed for the sake of "freedom." It is freedom that provides justification for concentration camps, military regimes, communist slavery, terrorism. More often than not the aim is to achieve a better, higher, more genuine freedom than the fraudulent pseudofreedom achieved through the uncensored press, unrestricted travel, elected parliaments, multiparty political life, an independent judiciary, guarantees against arbitrary arrests, and so on.

In a sense, we may think that this is a victory for the idea of freedom: nobody dares attack it under its name. In another sense it is a defeat in disguise: a victory for the word, a defeat for meaning. One might argue that there is no meaning attached to the word by a divine decree or by natural law and that there is nothing essentially wrong with giving slavery the name of "freedom" and to genocide the name of "liberation," as long as there is no confusion about what actually is meant. This, however, would be an intellectual self-deception. We cannot detach from the word "freedom" all the associations, however vague, which prevent people, even the most dedicated advocates of tyranny, from attacking it under its very name. Therefore, it is imperative that we not let the traditional meaning of the word be obscured and loaded with all sorts of goods and claims which, even if well justified in themselves, belong to another lexical category.

In defending the idea of freedom against all kinds of distortion and contamination and in preventing the noble word from being employed by totalitarian movements and ideologies, by actual or would-be despots, we ought to keep in mind a few simple truths, some of them semantic, others empirical.

First, freedom is a negative concept; it is defined by the scope of human activities which are *not* regulated by any law or restricted by violence. This implies:

Second, that freedom, as we know it, is always and inevitably restricted by the very nature of social life. "Total freedom," i.e., Robinson Crusoe's freedom, is an empty slogan. It is empty in the sense that it can never be implemented, but it is dangerous as well. The ideal of anarchists, implying the absence of law, would amount to the unrestricted tyranny of the strongest and so, by a curious *coincidentia oppositorum*, would mean the total abrogation of freedom. We do not know and we cannot even imagine unlimited freedom.

Third, there are many human aspirations which, though perfectly legitimate, do not belong to the definition of freedom and many forms of human suffering and deprivation which should not be defined as unfreedom. To have enough to eat is a natural human desire; however, it is an abuse of language to say that by having enough to eat I am "free from hunger." People can be free and hungry at the same time; they might be enslaved and have enough food. A useful test in investigating such cases is provided by the simple question: which human claims can be conceivably satisfied in prisons or in concentration camps? It is quite conceivable that in a concentration camp the inmates are "free from hunger" and "free from unemployment." It does not follow that they are free in any recognizable sense.

Fourth, from the concept of freedom itself nothing may be inferred about which limitations of freedom are desirable or condemnable in all imaginable conditions. Granted that all social organization limits our freedom and that freedom allows for gradation, the bare idea of freedom clearly defines nothing concerning the extent of socially justifiable unfreedom. Taxation, to take the simplest example, of whatever kind, imposes limitations on our freedom; it deprives us of choice in using our income. This does not mean that taxation should be abolished, yet it does not follow either that taxation is a special variety of freedom. It is a justifiable unfreedom. Clearly, however, in itself the idea of freedom provides us with no answer to the question as to which taxation system is recommendable in a given social situation.

Fifth, it is often the case that freedom clashes with other values people cherish and there is no simple formula for resolving such conflicts or for drawing the line of admissible compromises. It is notorious, in particular, that freedom and security limit each other. Perfect security can be provided only by an omnipotent (i.e., totalitarian) state which deprives individuals of responsibility for their lives by destroying their freedom. Any amount of freedom involves an amount of insecurity. If we believe that freedom is to be protected, we admit that it can never coexist with a perfect security. All measures whereby the welfare state alleviates the insecurity of individual life, however justifiable, necessarily limit the scope of freedom. This does not imply, again, that we should scrap them, but it does imply that we have to be aware of this collision.

This entails, *Sixth*, that there is no such thing as freedom without social cost. For the freedom we enjoy, we pay. However we might dislike pornography, it cannot be entirely eradicated in a society that enjoys freedom of the press. We have to admit that freedom of speech inevitably results in various absurd and harmful ideas being spread with impunity. Freedom of travel obviously makes the work of criminals and terrorists easier. This boils down to a common-sense platitude: we never have a choice between perfection and imperfection, only between various forms of imperfection. One may add, incidentally, that this is what Solzhenitsyn seems to be unable to grasp: he is appalled—often quite justifiably—at the sight of socially and psychologically disastrous effects of Western licentiousness without realizing that many of them are just the price those societies pay for their freedom.

Seventh, from the fact that freedom and unfreedom allow for gradation it does not follow that we may not make a qualitative distinction between a free and unfree social organization. A free society is not a society in which no limitations are imposed on freedom. Rather, perhaps the most useful way to identify a "free society" is to say that it is a society where conflicts may be openly expressed. This implies a number of institutional mechanisms built into the social fabric and usually associated with democratic constitutions. The expression "free society" is not proper in this context, to be sure: what we have in mind is a society in which *individuals* are free.

* * *

All the seven observations I have been trying to phrase deal with the concept of freedom which is applicable to individuals. May we use the same or analogous concept when talking about societies? It appears that it is possible. In this sense freedom means the same as sovereignty. Needless to say, the empirical connection between freedom of individuals and the sovereignty of social organisms is negative only: a society which is sovereign and which gives no freedom to its members is perfectly conceivable, and the examples abound. The concept of sovereignty, as we know, involves a number of special difficulties on which even the highly competent experts in international law do not necessarily agree and which I do not feel competent to discuss. It need only be mentioned that, in contrast to individual freedom, the notion of national sovereignty does not make obvious, a priori, who or what is legitimately the subject of sovereignty; any definition implying a decision of this question involves a value judgment. Ultimately, the decisions are made by the collective will.

In contrast to collective sovereignty, which is perhaps a matter of historical contingency, the freedom of individuals has—we may presume—an anthropological foundation. This is admittedly a doctrine which cannot be proved or disproved in the normal sense of the word "prove." And yet our hope that freedom is not going to be ultimately destroyed by the joint pressure of totalitarianism and of general bureaucratization of the world and indeed our very readiness to defend it depend crucially on our belief that the desire for freedom, for sovereign individual self-assertion in free choice, is not an accidental fancy of history, not a result of peculiar social conditions or a temporary by-product of specific economic life forms, of market mechanisms, but that it is rooted in the very quality of being human. It has repeatedly appeared to some prophets in our century that the social order which guarantees civil liberties and human rights is a sort of abnormal freak of history, a brief break to be replaced soon by a supposedly normal condition of collective life: despotism in one form or another. These gloomy predictions are, fortunately, nothing more than an arbitrary extrapolation of phenomena which we may notice right now, which, however, by no means deserve to be forged into a general philosophy of history.

Nevertheless, if these views receive credence on a large scale, this credence might put into movement a mechanism of a self-fulfilling prophecy by convincing us that our effort to resist and to fight against the totalitarian threat is in vain, because of the allegedly providential legislation; that we are fighting against the inevitable. This is what in fact the totalitarian ideology in its Marxist-Leninist version is unceasingly trying to do: it pretends to have discovered that in a natural sequence of modes of production "capitalism" (i.e., market economy) is bound to be replaced by "socialism," meaning the Soviet variant of slavery.

Beyond Empiricism

This ideological device, whereby the agents of totalitarian tyranny automatically become agents of historical destiny and of progress, is hardly ineffective, little as it can be supported by any rational examination of social changes.

There are, to be sure, various social forces powerfully resisting ideological and political pressure of totalitarianism and our hope that they will prove strong enough to prevent Western civilization from falling prey to barbarity is reasonably well-founded. This hope, however, would be enormously weakened, perhaps even doomed to failure if we abandoned our belief that the will to freedom is not a momentary whim of history, a contingent oddity, but that it is unremovably rooted in the very fiat whereby the human race was called to life, that it defines the condition in which our species is recognizably itself. If we think instead that it is conceivable for mankind to live happily in slavery, we can well imagine that all the glaring failures of totalitarianism are accidental and technical and that there is nothing wrong with trying to devise a corrected, faultless version in which people would have all their needs satisfied while functioning as state property, as in communist doctrine and practice. If we grant that freedom is not among the goods we really need, we might then think there is nothing incompatible with being state-owned and in bringing to fruition all our human potentialities.

On the other hand, on the assumption that the right to choose is a claim which makes up the very core of personal life and that that form of life which is specifically human is personal, the historical emergence of freedom embodied in its contemporary institutional forms, far from being a pathological deviation, is to be seen as a gradual maturation of an indestructible seed that no historical accidents could have either killed or produced. On this assumption, when we demand freedom as something due to us, we do not just express an arbitrary norm which a governmental body may deny or cancel with the same right or the same arbitrariness: we imply that our demand has a *fundamentum in re*, that it is the constitution of humanity rather than a groundless decision which makes our requirement valid.

Let me repeat: the presence of an anthropological foundation of the will to freedom and of the right of freedom is not an issue which could ever be conclusively settled by an empirical investigation. It is a philosophical issue but one of those—and there are many of this kind—we simply may not disregard or reject on the ground that they are insoluble according to the rules that govern scientific inquiry. We do not have the option of neutrality or of dismissal, because too much is at stake. We may not avoid a resolution—arbitrary as it might appear in scientific terms—because the issue is of utmost importance and by deciding one way or another we either assert our will to resist the totalitarian cancer or we say in substance that there are no legitimate reasons for such a resistance.

I leave aside the question which is not only obviously relevant to, but perhaps even crucial in, all discussions on this obscure subject: to what extent the assertion that the need for freedom is an anthropological constant depends—logically or historically—on the validity of our religious legacy. It need only be mentioned that if such a constant is indeed present in the very constitution of humanity it is not likely that it can be satisfactorily described in biological or etiological terms: orientation reflexes, neoteny, lack of rigid specialization, etc. The reason why it is not likely is that when we talk about the desire for freedom in the human species, we mean more than an empirical statement to the effect that men are actually unhappy if they have no choice; such a statement can always be refuted with the satirical "first law of sociology" of which I regrettably forgot the author and which says: some do, some don't. We have in mind a quasi-platonic, not empirical, presupposition about the *essentia* of being human and such an *essentia*, we ought to admit, may never be deduced from gathering data about human behavior. Identifying this *essentia* helps us answer not the question "How do humans behave?" but rather the logically prior question "What is it to be human?" The latter cannot be answered without a measure of arbitrariness and yet it has to be answered; whatever the answer might be, it is decisive and indispensable to our beliefs about how to distinguish between rights and wrongs in human affairs. If we think that the human species can be exhaustively described in etiological and biological categories, there is nothing wrong in asserting that an individual is simply a provisional wrapping of the genetic plasma; on the other hand, the very idea of personality is valid only on the contrary assumption that personality has an irreducible ontological status of its own and that it is creative by being able to choose. And the right to choose cannot be properly affirmed without this assumption.

The cause of freedom is not, then, philosophically neutral: in opting for freedom we take a philosophical—and not merely a political—position for which we may not claim to be capable of providing a sufficient scientific justification. This is why freedom in our culture is threatened not only by doctrines that directly endorse totalitarianism or any other form of slavery. It is threatened as well by the spirit of scientism. Scientism, in contrast to science, is a philosophical doctrine stating that cognitive value and indeed meaningfulness itself is granted to our thought by the proper application of procedures employed in modern empirical and mathematical sciences. Scientism itself is neither a part of science nor its logical conclusion or a logical condition; it is an arbitrary ideological position which we are entirely free to reject without questioning anything in the results or in the guiding norms of science.

Professor Kolakowski, Senior Research Fellow at All Souls College, Oxford University, is the author of *Husserl and the Search for Certitude, Geist und Ungeist,* and many other books on philosophy, politics, and history.

II.

FREEDOM AND THE MARKET

4.

Movement in the Market: Mobility and Economics in the Free Society

Paul Johnson

No student of history can doubt that, in the long run, mankind is moving towards greater individual freedom. Material progress depends on innovation and innovatory societies are characterized by a high degree of freedom. We have moved progressively from the collectivist communities of antiquity to a world in which the uniqueness of the individual is conceded, at least theoretically, and the universality of human rights is given formal recognition. Few regimes now officially deny the rights of man; virtually all admit, as a kind of self-evident truth, that freedom is a public good. Just as hypocrisy is the tribute vice pays to virtue, so constitutions embodying human rights are the homage which even the worst tyranny now feels obliged to lay at the feet of Freedom. Every petty despotism in Africa has its theoretical bill of rights, and the Soviet Union, though the most authoritarian and restrictive system of government ever devised, has a constitution of exemplary benevolence. Of course such documents are often, indeed usually, fraudulent. But the fact that they exist at all, that the genuflection to freedom is considered necessary even by tyrannies, is progress of a kind, an acknowledgement even by those who in practice deny it that freedom is a social good.

Where we tend to go wrong is in our attempt to distinguish between different aspects of freedom and to adjudicate between them, thus deciding that some freedoms are necessary, others less so. We speak of freedom of speech, of worship, of trade, of movement, and so on, as though there were more, and less, valuable kinds of freedom: a hierarchy of freedom. I believe these distinctions are fundamentally false and that freedom is indivisible: all freedoms are subsumed in the freedom to choose, the notion that we are endowed by God with free will and that freedom of choice lies with the individual, not society, though the individual can delegate his power to assemblies and parliaments and congresses.

In particular, I believe that one of the cardinal errors of modern times, an error of which I was guilty for a quarter of a century while a socialist, is the belief that one can distinguish between political and economic freedom. I used to accept, as indeed all democratic socialists must accept, that political and economic freedom were quite different, that you could preserve, even enhance, the one by restricting the other. I used to think that you could limit economic freedom very severely, while leaving political freedom intact. I no longer believe that to be true, or even that it is possible to make such a distinction. Both from the study of history, and from observation of the contemporary world, it has become clear to me that the destruction of economic freedom leads inevitably to the destruction of political freedom. The opposite is true as well: for where political freedom no longer exists, it is hard to maintain economic freedom for long. The process also works in reverse: once freedom of trade is acquired by large numbers of individuals, as it was in ancient Greece in the 8th-6th centuries B.C., free political institutions also emerge quite rapidly. Or again, it is no accident that the expansion of economic freedom in the 18th century, which created the Industrial Revolution, was also the progenitor of parliamentary democracy and universal suffrage. The truth is that all the so-called "freedoms" are aspects of one fundamental freedom which is based on the proposition that the individual is usually a better judge of his interests than any collective. Once one aspect of this freedom is secured, the others accrue in time; once one aspect is lost, the others tend to disappear in due course.

I want to illustrate this proposition, and in so doing argue the case for the social benefits of freedom, by dwelling on two particular aspects of freedom: the freedom of the market and the freedom of movement, two aspects which are indeed closely connected, since neither can function effectively without the other.

The social benefits of the free market are, of course, often denied. They are denied especially by many intellectuals and academics in the West. Such people would go to the stake on behalf of the freedom to seek and acquire knowledge. Yet they would severely restrict the operation of the free market, denouncing it variously as "the law of the jungle," "Thatcherism", "Reaganomics," "Friedmanism" and so on. Yet, in fact the market has nothing to do with the jungle. It is essentially a very sophisticated knowledge system, a system whereby information is acquired and disseminated. Let me explain. One of the most common of human fallacies is the assumption that goods have a fixed or absolute value, and that those who make or grow them have a unique entitlement to that value. The assumption, termed "the Physical Fallacy," treats any kind of middleman or nonproducer as an obnoxious parasite. This assumption is basic to Marx's labor theory of value and, indeed, to his detestation of the bourgeoisie as opposed to the proletariat, whom he identified as the only genuine producers of value. The physical fallacy is shared by most crude economic thinkers, such as the old-fashioned moralists who preach the doctrine of the "just price" and who condemn lending at interest as "usury." Such moralists anticipated Marx in condemning the bourgeois middleman as antisocial, and sought to relegate such roles to the Jews, who were condemned already. Marx, and still more Lenin, broadened the category of condemnation to include the entire middle class: it was not merely the Jews who were to blame for the economic ills of society but the bourgeoisie as a whole. Hence Lenin's dictum that "anti-Semitism is the socialism of fools."

I was made aware of the consequences of the physical fallacy when I visited Indonesia in the twilight of the obnoxious Sukarno regime. Sukarno, a socialist *and* a racist, had persecuted the minority Chinese business community to the point that it was no longer able to function. As a result, in the capital of Djakarta there was virtually nothing to eat. Less than 100 miles away, as I saw for myself, villages were producing fruit, vegetables and meat in abundance, and it was rotting unsold. The Chinese traders who ran the trucks which carried the food from villages to the capital had been hounded off the scene, and no

Movement in the Market

one had yet been able to take their place. So the market system did not function.

The truth is, there is no such thing as absolute value in goods. It all depends on where and when those goods can be found. Goods in the wrong place at the wrong time or the right place at the wrong time or the wrong place at the right time have a diminished value or, if perishable, no value at all. The essential function of the market is to change the location of goods in space and time, and it is location and timing which determine value and price. Getting the location and time right is a highly professional business exacting penalties for misjudgment or incompetence that are at least as severe as those in manufacturing and farming. The middleman is no more a parasite than the physical producer.

Now, it is a matter of historical record and actual observation that free-market systems are more effective at getting the location and timing right, and so at delivering the goods, than collectivist ones. Why, exactly?

Why, 65 years after the collectivist revolution, does the Soviet Union, with more land under cultivation than any other nation on earth, experience chronic food shortages, during which it is forced to avail itself of surpluses produced by the market economies of the United States, Canada, Australia and Europe? Why are the Soviet Union and other countries with nonmarket economies forced to employ rationing of most consumer goods, rationing them either by time (the ubiquitous line or queue) or by occupation (shops selling scarce goods open only to party functionaries or those with access to foreign currency)?

One can provide many explanations, but they all amount to the same thing. Economic efficiency is the consequence of making the right decisions. And making decisions correctly depends on access to accurate knowledge. And this is essentially what the free-market system provides. The market is a natural device for the speedy conveyance of cheap, accurate and objective information. Since there is no absolute value in goods, the free market will tell you the exact going price and the level of demand of anything in any place and at any time within the society allowing it to function. It is speedy because the market functions around the clock all over the world, cheap because it is the free by-product of buying and selling, accurate because it is based upon an endless multiplicity of real transactions, and objective because the market is not an institution with a purpose or an ideology but a simple mirror of human desires in all their nakedness.

Wherever the market provides access to this quality of information, the quality of decision-making will improve accordingly. This will in turn be reflected in economic performance and so in social benefit. The market is hence a knowledge system. That is one reason why the market has been the biggest single utilizer of modern electronic means of communication, thus enormously increasing the celerity with which it distributes knowledge across the world and so increasing the efficiency of its performance. This knowledge is free, unbiased and uncensored: the free access to knowledge is as important to the functioning of the market as it is to any university or newspaper or writer of books. The moment governments start to intervene in the market, for whatever reason (and there may be good ones), the volume and quality of the information declines. The information ceases to be wholly objective because it tends to reflect the subjective views of the interventionists. So the market begins to give out false or misleading signals—indeed, beyond a certain point of intervention it does not give out signals at all, and a great darkness and silence descends. I remember a leading Polish planner in Warsaw complaining to me—it was during a particularly "Stalinist" period—that Poland's planners no longer really knew the cost of any of the products they were making, which industries, let alone which individual factories, were operating efficiently, or who among their managers ought to be promoted or sacked. As he put it, "Without market criteria, we are without yardsticks of success or failure." Of course in the very long term success or failure *will* manifest themselves even in a totally controlled economy, first in the form of queues, then in the form of riots—as we have, indeed, seen in Poland. The social virtue of the market is that it provides not only accurate information for decision-making but instant feedback after the decisions are made, so that it is not merely an early-warning system for catastrophe but a continuous warning system which allows us to monitor the effects of decisions from day to day and correct them accordingly.

Hence, government restrictions on the market are forms of censorship, suppressions of truth, or attempts to poison wells. They are forms of rigging: attempts to bias the market in favor of some group or purpose (which may be admirable) to the disadvantage of another. Now, when private individuals capture and rig a market, we recognize the process for the evil it is. When the Hunt brothers tried to control the silver market in 1980, what a storm of reprobation they aroused! Their failure and the huge loss they incurred were universally hailed as a great moral example to us all—and proof that there is some justice in this world. Yet what the Hunts attempted, once in a lifetime, governments do every day. And whereas the Hunts ignominiously failed, governments succeed because they possess something which the Hunts, with all their vast resources, conspicuously lacked—statutory power. Government rigging, government suppression of market freedom and so of truth, is legal.

Suppose the Hunts had succeeded. The most important effect would have been to cast an impenetrable veil over the true (i.e., the market) value of silver. You may think this particular bit of knowledge is unimportant. Let us therefore turn to those areas everyone recognizes as important. In communications, for instance, both the British and the U.S. governments limit market freedom by imposing state monopolies in mail. Market signals about the best way of running a mail service are silenced, because only one is permitted. In 1980, the General Secretary of the British postal workers' union, which has a deep vested interest in the rigged mail market, boasted that he had alerted all his members to spot and report for prosecution any British firms which were taking their circulars in bulk to Holland and mailing them there. The fact that it is cheaper to take the mail to Holland and post it there for delivery in Britain is a fearful condemnation of the British postal monopoly. Here the market was struggling to give us a piece of information highly unfavorable to the riggers. So they promptly enlist an army of spies and informers to have that information suppressed by law.

This restriction of knowledge and freedom in the market takes many forms. Both the American and British governments limit the free market in TV and radio broadcasting by an enormous carving-up of franchises, that is, through the creation of absolute or quasi-monopolies, administered in authoritarian fashion by the Federal Communications Commission and the Independent Broadcasting Authority. As a result, nobody in either country knows which is the most efficient, cheap, or popular form of broadcasting. The free-market solution is to award contracts or franchises to the highest bidders: then the viewing public has a chance of getting the program they want rather than what they are served up by the riggers. The new cable system gives them that chance, but attempts are being made in Britain to rig that. The freedom of the newspaper market is limited in a different way by the existence of labor monopolies. It is a curious fact that whereas the U.S. and Britain have enacted extensive antimonopoly and antitrust legislation, both permit labor monopolies to flourish. As a result, New York, one of the greatest and richest cities on earth, has only three daily newspapers. London is luckier with ten, but many of them are in precarious straits because of the labor monopoly. Granted the new electronic technology, both cities ought to have dozens of papers, perhaps even scores—just as both (that is, if the riggers are held at bay) will soon have scores of cable TV channels.

In transportation interference with the freedom of the market is infinitely complex. Let me give you one example. In 1980, the American Enterprise Institute published a survey proving beyond any reasonable doubt that Amtrack never could or would make money. A couple of years ago, the chairman of British Rail told me that there was no possibility of the London commuter and Southeast Region services ever making money—of ever failing, indeed, to incur an enormous loss—and that if he were running a private company he would shut them down tomorrow. But of course the government would permit no such thing. You may say: "And quite right too!" But how do you *know*? Here is a case in which the free-market system of knowledge may be trying to tell us something: that we can get along without railroads, that the age of the rail is over. But we cannot put this information to the test because the response of the riggers is to suppress the message. So new systems of commuter transport do not evolve, and society is thereby impoverished. I suppose we are lucky, in a way, that the railroad came before Western governments learned how to rig the transportation market—otherwise we might still be subsidizing stagecoaches.

Nowhere is government rigging and suppressing of knowledge more prevalent and nowhere is it more socially baneful than in the energy market. Nearly every country is making a mess of its energy policy because nowhere is the market allowed freely to tell us the truth, the whole truth, and nothing but the truth. Coal, oil, shale oil, natural gas, wind and water, nuclear power, other forms of energy yet undreamed of but waiting to be tapped—and the range of options and the permutations within them is almost infinite. It is beyond the wit of any government, composed though it may be of disinterested geniuses—a cabinet of Einsteins—to get right the complex decisions and choices which will be justified in 10, 20, or 50 years. In the energy field, perhaps more than in any other, only the free market—an infinite natural computer, which in the long run has the infallibility of nature itself—can produce the continuous stream of information on which investment decisions should be made and monitored. Yet it is in this field above all that governments consistently falsify and distort the information by refusing to allow the market to operate freely.

For as a system of knowledge the market arrives at conclusions that are socially just, on balance, because it is essentially democratic. In elections, we vote with our pen every two or four or five years. That is what the freedom to vote means. But in the free market we vote with our purses in the shops every day of our lives. We vote with our pennies every day we buy a newspaper and this exercises some control over the press tycoons. We vote with our fingers when we turn the knob of our TV set. We vote on transportation policies every day by deciding how we get to work. We vote about energy policy every winter by deciding how to heat our homes. The greater the range of choice in all these matters—the less governmental interference, benevolent or otherwise, in the market—the greater the measure of true freedom and democracy we enjoy and the bigger the harvest of social benefit in terms of increased efficiency.

We also, and let us never forget it, vote with our feet, by deciding where we will live and under what authority we will place ourselves. As I have said, freedom is indivisible, but perhaps the purest expression of freedom is freedom of movement. And the most striking symbol of the denial of freedom is the Berlin Wall, a barrier erected not for defense, not to keep enemies out, but solely to prevent ordinary people from voting with their feet. Freedom of movement has to be suppressed by tyrannies because it is the ultimate verdict on the system. And the free movement of people, like the movement of goods in a free market, tells us the truth about the world. It tells us what ordinary people think. Marxist historians, and indeed many non-Marxist historians, have presented the coming of industrial capitalism as a great human misfortune. But what was the verdict of ordinary people, the social verdict? Industrial capitalism from the very start received the demonstrable approbation of the masses. Most of them could not vote in the ballot box, but they voted in a far more positive manner with their feet. The poorest member of society values political freedom as much as the richest, in my opinion. But the freedom he values as most meaningful is the freedom to sell his labor and skill in the open market. In rural society he did not possess such freedom. The factory system, however harsh it may have been, gave it to him. It allowed ordinary people to move from status to contract, from a stationary place in a static society, with tied cottages and semiconscript labor, to a mobile place in a dynamic one. That is why men voted for industrial capitalism with their feet by surging from the countryside into the towns, first in Britain and then throughout Europe. Tens of millions of European peasants, decade after decade, moved across the Atlantic in pursuit of that same freedom, from semifeudal estates and small holdings in Ireland, Poland, Germany, Austria-Hungary, Russia, Italy, and Scandinavia to the mines and factories and workshops of New York, Chicago, Detroit, Pittsburgh, Cleveland, to Buenos Aires, Rio de Janeiro, and São Paulo. They voted for industrial capitalism with their feet—for the free market in fact—not only because they felt in their bones that it meant a modest prosperity for their descendants—and they have been proved right in that—but because it meant a new freedom for themselves.

That great 19th-century movement of peoples has continued throughout the 20th. Wherever they can do so, and many totalitarian governments try to prevent them, peasants have been moving into the cities—in China, Southeast Asia, India, and throughout Africa and Latin America. It is significant that the most evil tyrannies of our time have denied freedom of movement by fighting against this process. Stalin's collectivization of the peasants—which cost the lives of 20 million of them—was essentially a corralling process, a restriction not merely of the free market but of feet-voting. The worst regimes of the last few years, in Cambodia and Vietnam, have sought to reverse the process by actually driving city dwellers, by the compulsion of mass-murder and terror, back into the countryside to be dragooned into rural collectives.

All forms of freedom bring social benefit, but it is my contention that freedom of movement, the purest expression of freedom, is the most socially beneficial because it is the key to all forms of dynamism, not least economic dynamism. Why is Western civilization so successful? Because its central characteristic is dynamism. Some irresistible force—perhaps the obsession with time instilled by Christian ethical teaching—impels continuous forward motion. Western man is a restless creature, which is why Thomas Hobbes compares existence to a race in his *Leviathan*. Felicity is the state of mind of those who are in front. But there is no finish line. The point of life is to be in the race: "There is no such thing as perpetual tranquility of mind while we live here, because life itself is but motion and can never be without desire, or without fear, no more than without sense . . . there can be no contentment but in proceeding."

That is the nature of man, and explains why freedom of movement is so essential to personal content, as well as to social efficiency. Dynamic economies move forward not merely in time but in place. Let me give you a theorem: dislocation and relocation are essential to growth. What do I mean by this? That dynamism involves the constant movement of people, the resiting of industrial centers and the perpetual restructuring of communications, thus effecting the decay of leading economic sectors—as Professor Rostow terms them—and the rise of new ones. Above all, economic history shows the constant switching of geographical emphasis from one area of expansion to another.

The ancient Greeks had a saying: "There was a Pylos before Pylos, and another Pylos before that." What they meant was that the Pylos then extant, the city of the Homeric hero Nestor, was merely the latest of a series, the smoking ruins of each earlier citadel serving as foundations for the next, as the free play of economic, political, and military forces thrust up and in turn demolished races, kingdoms, dynasties. On the site of Troy, archaeologists have been able to distinguish thirteen distinct cities, stretching over two millennia, with Homer's Troy constituting VIIb—about the middle. Similarly, cities fell forever silent, as history, economics, but above all people moved on. When the weeds finally closed over Troy, Byzantium began to rise. Thebes decayed—but Athens prospered. Mycenae fell to dust—but Sparta arose. The process goes on throughout antiquity, on an ever-broadening scale, into the Dark and Middle Ages. Enormous cities like Antioch became haunted ruins. Others, like Aquilaea, disappeared almost without trace. In their place, human enterprise and economic change conjured out of the earth new metropolises, first Venice, then Genoa, Pisa, and Florence, then Antwerp, Amsterdam, London, New York, and so on. There is growth always, but the focus of fastest growth is constantly changing, moving on. And the essence of this dynamism is freedom of movement.

In our own lifetime, we have been able to observe this beneficent relocating process at work. In the 1940s and the 1950s, the wonder of the world economy was the United States, first the arsenal of the Allied war effort, then the matrix of postwar recovery through the Marshall Plan, and then an exemplar to the world in the decade of Eisenhower prosperity, when all the world wanted dollars. In the late 1950s and 1960s, the emphasis shifted to Western Europe as the *Wirtshaftwunder* got into stride and the European Economic Community became the model of rational cooperation, high investment, and rapid growth. Then in the 1960s, the 1970s, and into the 1980s the focus of economic development has switched to the rim of the Pacific, with Japan leading the way with phenomenal rates of capital accumulation, productivity increases, and GNP growth—but with a whole cluster of Asian economies from South Korea to Taiwan and Singapore with equal or higher growth rates, and with the dynamism of the Pacific economy stimulating economic activity as far apart as Australia, Alaska, the Northwestern Pacific states, California, Mexico, and Chile.

I stress freedom of movement because movement seems to go to the very heart of this economic growth. Even though the emigration barriers have gone up, as they have done increasingly since the 1920s, especially in the last three decades, internal migrations continue, of peasants into towns, of workers from low- to high-growth areas. The more the movement, the greater the growth. Federal Germany's rapid growth was made possible by the huge movement of refugees from German Poland across the Oder-Neisse line and then into West Germany. The success of Gaullist France was due both to a general movement of peasants into industrial areas and to the growth of vast new industries in south-central France, once largely an agricultural preserve. Japan's upsurge is essentially a movement of manpower—and womanpower—from rural to urban areas, a pattern repeated in South Korea. The rise of Hong Kong, Taiwan, and Singapore as major entreneurial economies springs from their copious drawing on the inexhaustible rural manpower of mainland China.

Equally, the continuing dynamism of the American economy is ensured by internal movements. In the 1940s, the Northeastern United States, known to geographers as the "core area" of the economy, with only 8 percent of the land area, had 43 percent of the population and a massive 68 percent of the manufacturing employment. In the 20 years 1940-60, the North was still gaining population—2 million net by migration, while the South lost 3.5 million. But the North's gain was low-income and largely unskilled blacks. It was already suffering a net loss of whites. Towards the end of the 1960s the turnabout took place and accelerated swiftly in the 1970s. In the years 1970-77, the North lost 2.4 million by migration, while the South experienced a net gain of 3.4 million, most of them skilled workers. Regional variations in income—once heavily in favor of the core area—began to diminish. By the late 1970s they had virtually disappeared, and by the very early 1980s average incomes in the old core area were below the national average. This mirrored and reflected a switch in investment from North to South. The old core area's share of American manufacturing employment fell from 66 percent in 1950 to 50 percent in 1977 and is now not much above 40 percent. Meanwhile the South's share rose from 20 percent to nearly 40 percent.

We have here a perfect illustration of freedom of movement allowing the economy to adjust to new pressures and challenges. The shift was and is essentially from the Frost Belt to the Sun Belt and, in a period when energy costs rose very fast, reflected a growing differential in heating costs. Second, the growth of the interstate highway system made the geographical concentration which favored the old core area less significant. Third, the higher land costs in the concentrated core area promoted immigration to the South and West. Fourth, there is the attraction of natural resources in the South and West. Finally, there is the lure of lower labor costs, since the North's far heavier unionization entails the inevitable consequences of restrictive practices and overmanning. Most states in the new growth areas have right-to-work laws which make closed or union shops illegal.

Because the United States has freedom of movement for both labor and capital, society has been able to adjust to economic changes with reasonable speed and efficiency. The most dynamic parts of the American economy are now to be found in California and the West Coast generally, in the Mountain states, and in Texas and the South. But it is a curious fact that many American opinion-formers represent this swing of the economic center of gravity as a "problem" demanding intervention by the Federal government. Of course it is true that most of America's more influential newspapers, newsmagazines, and TV networks are centered in the old core area—in itself a dangerous anomaly—and that the old core area therefore receives attention and sympathy. The burgeoning prosperity of the South and West is accordingly presented as a source of envy, and even a manifestation of some kind of injustice, rather than a cause for congratulation that dynamic forces are still at work in the U.S.

In a rational society, the resources of government should be deployed, if at all, to reinforce success, to speed, facilitate, and strengthen the natural forces of economic growth. The notion that they should be used to reinforce failure, to resist success, and to hold back the inexorable and natural pressure of history, demography, and technology seems foolish in the extreme. Yet in modern social democracies that is precisely what governments tend to do. This was implicit in Roosevelt's New Deal, in Lyndon Johnson's Great Society program and in much of the Federal legislation of the 1970s.

Such efforts are bound to end in failure, as the experience of Britain indicates. There the Industrial Revolution produced the first great economic movement of modern times—the switch of the economic center of gravity from the Southeast to the midlands and the North. It continued through most of the 19th century, then spent itself. In the early decades of the 20th century there were already signs of a reversal. The result, even before 1914, was the initiation of a "regional policy" formulated as government efforts to redress the balance of nature and freeze the existing economic structure. Such efforts have continued right up to the present at steadily increasing cost and involving a growing complexity of bureaucratic arrangements. Failure has been steadily reinforced for more than half a century. The results are negligible. The old industrial core areas are no better off relative to the rest of the country: on the contrary, their decline has continued, even accelerated. No amount of subsidy has enabled them to recover their old economic dynamism. They consume wealth rather than create it. The American experience is shorter but already suggests exactly the same results. New York and Massachusetts, the old core industrial states whose "problems" have received the most attention—they contain the highest concentration of media and academic institutions—and therefore the most Federal dollars, have in fact the worst performance figures.

But if regional support programs are ineffective, they are not without consequences. To reinforce failure is to jeopardize success. These programs, involving vast expenditure, increase the general level of taxation and the size, activities, and borrowing of government, all to the disadvantage of the genuine growth areas. The prosperous Southeast in Britain, the prosperous South and West in America, have had to carry the main burden of a futile attempt to reverse the course of history and in so doing have seen their own chances of survival endangered. Even those who live in the decaying areas are injured, for they are encouraged to entertain false hopes and so are discouraged from taking steps themselves. Like ancient Judah, they rely "upon the staff of this broken reed"—the state—"on which, if a man lean, it will go into his hand, and pierce it" (2 Kings 18:21). It is significant that, all forms of subsidy having failed, the form of government action now being advocated on both sides of the Atlantic is the creation in depressed areas of "free zones," where the normal activities of government benevolence are, as it were, suspended, and what is termed "a Hong Kong solution" is made possible. What an unwitting testimony to the social benefits of freedom! I suspect such schemes will not work, for they will be done half-heartedly, as is already clear in the British experiment. For they enshrine a fundamental logical inconsistency. If to be free of government regulation is an overall economic advantage, as such schemes implicitly concede, why should they be suspended on a temporary and limited basis only? Why should they not be scrapped for good, and everywhere, so that the entire country may benefit permanently? Is not the mere notion of regulation-free areas an unspoken condemnation of the entire process whereby government tries to resist natural economic movements which are deeply rooted in the freedom of individual choice?

In this essay I have discussed the social benefits of only two aspects of freedom—knowledge and movement—and only in their materialistic aspects. But the true benefits of freedom are metaphysical. As I have said, freedom is not truly divisible, because if it is diminished in one aspect it is, sooner or later, diminished in others. And it nourishes not just the body, but the spirit. For freedom in its essence is the right of the individual to choose, for himself, between good and evil, the right to exercise his conscience. And the individual conscience is not only, in the end, the source of all social benefit, it is the foundation of human society itself. For humans without consciences are not a society at all: merely a congregation of clever animals.

Mr. Johnson, author of *Enemies of Society, Modern Times* and *Journey into Chaos,* was the inaugural holder of the DeWitt Wallace Chair in Communications in a Free Society at the American Enterprise Institute.

5.

The Profits of Freedom: Investing in the Defense of Business

Arthur Shenfield

Business is the product of freedom. What business does in free societies is in some measure simulated or paralleled in unfree societies by economic planners and bureaucrats, but such people would repudiate the appellation of "businessmen," nor would we describe them by that name. The function of businessmen in a free society is to serve the people with the goods and services which they, the people, freely choose for the satisfaction of their wants (subject to certain constraints to be discussed later). The function of economic planners and bureaucrats in an unfree society is to harness the people to the production of what they, not the people, require, and to distribute what they judge it is possible or politic to let the people have.

We observe this difference in the relatively free societies of the West when we see any business which appears to us, rightly or wrongly, to have power over the consumers whom it supplies, rather than being subject to their independent demands. If such a business is not called a public utility, its power or conduct appears to us to be contrary to the basic rule which should govern private enterprise, and we demand action, perhaps by antitrust law or perhaps otherwise, to make it conform to the governance of the free market. If it is held to be a public utility, we declare it to be an exception to governance by the free market, and so we seek to subordinate it to the interests of the people by other devices. In either case we display a fundamental belief in the principle that business exists to serve the people, not vice versa. I must hasten to say here in parenthesis that we often imagine that business has power over the consumers when it does not, but such an error of fact does not derogate from the validity of the principle to which we adhere. Similarly, the devices which we employ to regulate public utilities may be ineffective or counterproductive, but here again such failure does not derogate from the validity of our principle. By contrast, we know perfectly well that this principle does not, and cannot, apply to those who organize the production of goods and services in unfree societies.

We also observe the difference in our relatively free societies when we contemplate the provision of goods or services by the government. We may declare that the minions of the government are our servants, but unless we rebel and restore provision by private enterprise, we soon resign ourselves to the fact that the government will not aim to satisfy our wants as effectively as does private business. For we know that politicians and bureaucrats are by nature different from businessmen.

That business is the product of freedom is demonstrated by its history. In the long centuries leading to

The Profits of Freedom

the liberties of the 18th and 19th centuries, it was merchants who were most active in dissolving the static order of feudalism. By one device or another medieval towns obtained charters of freedom, which enabled them to build markets and spread market behavior, without which the modern world could not have come into existence. Even if, like Venice and Genoa, mercantile towns themselves became states and perhaps also mini-empires, their mercantile operations rested on, and promoted, a goodly measure of freedom for individual merchants. It is of course true that for many centuries merchants themselves maintained policies of regulation which limited the freedom of markets. It is also true that kings and other overlords often took a financial interest in mercantile operations, even if only by way of taxation or simple extortion, and that, hence, merchants might often be in association with despotic rulers. It is further true that the mercantilist system which immediately preceded the modern business era, and considerable elements of which have survived to this day, made trade an instrument of state power and aggrandizement. And still further it is true that in our day businessmen frequently show that they are ready to exchange part of their freedom (and a fortiori the freedom of their customers) for governmental favors, and that once in possession of those favors they present a hostile face to other businessmen who seek to enter their preserves.

Nevertheless, the ideas of freedom could never have developed without the rise of business, even if businessmen themselves may never have acquired more than an imperfect understanding of those ideas. It was no accident that the ideas of freedom grew to maturity most effectively in the Netherlands and in Britain or that in the 17th-century struggle between King and Parliament, from which modern ideas of constitutional government arose, the city of London was the bastion of the Parliamentary forces. The Virginia-New England combination which produced the independence of America and the unmatched wisdom of her Constitution, was not simply an alliance of landowners and merchants. For the scholarly gentlemen and lawyers of Virginia also had substantial interests in trade and had no difficulty in joining the merchants of New England in fostering a general interest in trade. Thus, business was not only the product of freedom. It was also a powerful agency for the spread and further development of the freedom from whose loins it sprang.

It was not only freedom which went hand in hand with the development of business. Although the ethical standards of business are commonly held in low regard, there have been few forces in human history which have exerted a more elevating influence upon human behavior. Adam Smith noted in *The Wealth of Nations* that men in all walks of life kept their word to each other more honorably in Holland than in England, and more in England than in his own Scotland. He attributed this to the fact that in his day the Dutch were a more mercantile people than the English, and the English more than the Scots; for business thrives where men learn to adhere to the sanctity of contract, and withers away where they do not. By the side of mercantile sanctity of contract, aristocratic noblesse oblige, however admirable in other respects, was a poor guardian of the reliability of a man's word. Furthermore, states themselves began to adhere to the sanctity of contract—only partially among themselves but more completely in their dealings with their citizens—in parallel with the rise to ascendancy of business and business principles. Thus, whereas emperors, kings, and lesser potentates in the precapitalist world habitually found reason to break their word to each other and to deal dishonestly with their creditors and their peoples, in the 19th century only states on the fringe of civilization defaulted on their loans or defrauded their citizens by the debasement of their currency. Now in the 20th century, with the weakening of the principles or conventions engendered by business, even states of high standing resort to the debasement of their currency, deliberately raising loans from their citizens which they know they will repay only in depreciated money.

Of course, sanctity of contract is only one expression of the numerous ways in which the life of business has on balance produced powerful civilizing forces. Consider, for example, the all-pervasive cruelties of precapitalist societies and of the postcapitalist socialist societies of our day. Consider the significance of the fundamental change wrought by the business-oriented society in the ways men seek to become rich. For millennia the prevailing way to become rich was to seize men's bodies or land, and in essentials this has been revived in our day by the rulers of our contemporary totalitarian societies. For the first time in human history the life of business, even though itself once involved in the seizure of men's bodies, led men to see that the most effective way to become rich was to serve man's wants abundantly, above all the wants of the masses rather than the wants of elites. From this discovery, even though constantly derided by "superior" persons who see nothing in the service of mass wants but the debasement of culture, there has sprouted a wide array of liberating and elevating forces.

In the 20th century the most powerful influences at work on men's minds have been collectivist in character. State welfare, state regulation, state intervention, state direction, state control or ownership—all these in their various forms and disguises, and in various degrees—have gripped men's minds and gained widespread approval. In all cases the effect has been to propel people into a servile condition. Where there is still a substantial legacy of free institutions, the collectivist drive has had to meet significant resistance. Yet even in these cases the élan has been mainly with the attack, not with the defense. As Hayek has said,

> We are still as free as we are because certain traditional but rapidly vanishing prejudices have impeded the process by which the inherent logic of the changes we have already made tends to assert itself in an ever-widening field. In the present state of opinion the ultimate victory of totalitarianism would indeed be no more than the final victory of the ideas already dominant in the intellectual sphere over a merely traditional resistance.[1]

But nowhere does collectivism deliver what it promises. So far from becoming happy, contented, and proud of what their mentors have wrought, the people in the still relatively free West become bemused, discontented, fractious, demanding, and hypercritical of their society and its institutions. As yet only a few see with clarity that the malady is collectivism itself. A large and growing number half-perceive it, but they do not yet have the stomach for resolute resistance to collectivism, mainly because they are still enticed by particular promises of benefits which they hope will come to them, even while

---

[1] *Law, Legislation and Liberty,* vol. 1 (Chicago: University of Chicago Press, 1973), p. 62.

sensing that the system as a whole is bankrupt and fraudulent. A substantial number still believe that there is a collectivist cure for every ill, and that if performance has fallen short of promise, it is because the state has not had enough power for its necessary tasks. In their view the remedy for the failure of collectivism is more collectivism.

In this situation the business community could have a key role to play. For though freedom has much greater value than abundance, Providence has so ordered the world that the two go together. Since it is the task and achievement of business to organize the abundance and since at the same time it is best equipped to do so in freedom, it ought to be a powerful healing force for the bemused victims of the collectivist malady. Regrettably, it has to be acknowledged that in fact businessmen for the most part display attitudes and behavior which are too confused and equivocal to enable them to become the healing force which they should be. Partly they side with their critics and enemies. Partly they behave in ways which they think serve their interests but in fact undermine them. And partly they defend themselves against their critics and enemies in ways which are often ill-considered or inept. Hence, it is a prime task of those who champion freedom and know how much the free society needs to embody a healthy, vigorous business system to aid the business community to raise its defenses to an elevated and effective level.

How do businessmen side with their enemies? Consider the following. First, in societies with a legacy of freedom, the aim of collectivists is often the mixed economy. They concede merit to a certain measure, perhaps even a large measure, of private enterprise, as long as the commanding heights of the economy are in governmental hands, and usually also as long as private enterprise submits when required to some overall governmental regulation or direction. Many businessmen find this to be a seductive package. They are gratified by the concession of the right of private enterprise to exist and still more by what appears to be an offer of partnership with the government, whose aura of prestige and power impresses them. To be invited to the Presidential or Prime Ministerial residence for consultation of weighty economic matters (of which neither they nor their hosts may have much understanding) raises their self-esteem considerably. More important still, since businessmen are generally not economists, philosophers, or analytical thinkers (except within the narrow range of their business tasks, where their insight may be highly acute), they tend to be influenced by the climate of opinion as much as the general public, except where that opinion is clearly and directly hostile to business. Therefore they will swallow the alleged need for governmental control or direction as readily as the general public does, except where such control or direction pinches their individual shoes.

But the most conspicuous feature of the mixed economy is its instability. The mixture does not stay put. If, as is usually the case, the results are unsatisfactory, collectivists declare that the governmental share in the mixture must be increased. If, as is occasionally the case, the public sector appears to be successful (only appears, because its full costs or full effects may be unseen or camouflaged), then once again the claim is for more of it. Either way the collectivist pressure is for more collectivism.

If, as in most Western European countries, the public sector includes a substantial element of nationalized industry, this trend of collectivist pressure is obvious. If, as in the United States, the public element mainly takes the form of regulation, the tendency was until recently towards the spread of regulation into further fields. That at last a reaction has set in against regulation is *not* mainly due to intelligent resistance by the business community. Witness the determined resistance of the trucking industry to its proposed liberation from Interstate Commerce Commission regulation. Witness the resistance of the great majority of the airline companies to the dismantling of the Civil Aeronautics Board when it was first mooted. Witness the ready approval of, perhaps enthusiasm for, Mr. Nixon's wage and price controls shown by the representative business organizations in 1971.

Second, see how the business community tends to swallow some of the prescriptions of its critics and enemies. Take the case of the so-called social responsibility of business. The true social responsibility of business in a free society is to produce the goods and services required by the people in such a manner as to give them the best possible value for their money, subject to the constraint that the behavior of business should be honorable as well as lawful and efficient. Honorable behavior goes above and beyond mere legality. Thus, for example, one is not obliged to deal with employees, suppliers, customers, or creditors solely according to the strict requirements of one's contractual rights and obligations. Honorable conduct may go above and beyond precise contractual requirements. Or, as a further example, if pornography is held by the courts to be lawful, one is not thereby obliged to serve the wants of pornography peddlers. Honorable conduct in sport implies abiding not only by the rules of the game but also by the canons of sportsmanship. So, too, with modifications, in business. Of course the parameters of honorable business behavior can never be precisely determined. They are flexible and necessarily vary with personal judgment, and a businessman ought not to be castigated because in a given instance he judges that it is honorable to adhere solely to the strict requirements of the law. But though the boundaries of honorable behavior may be fuzzy in practice, the concept of honorable behavior is clear enough.

Contrast with this the concept of the social responsibility of business favored by the critics and enemies of business. In their view it is a prime function of business to apply its resources to the solution of social problems. Accordingly business should deal with poverty, unemployment, bad housing, even crime, over and above the satisfaction of the people's wants. There is no more perverse or destructive a prescription for business than this. Yet many businessmen, perhaps out of conviction or perhaps out of weakness, accept it. Consider a case in which we all understand this fallacy. Mr. George Steinbrenner is the (principal) owner of the New York Yankees. The Yankees' home is in the Bronx. As everyone knows, the Bronx is afflicted by some of the most grievous social maladies in the United States. Mr. Steinbrenner has numerous critics, perhaps even enemies. But no one criticizes him because he does not solve the social problems of the Bronx. We understand that his function is a different one, namely to serve the wants of baseball fans. If, however, he were a prominent industrial employer in the Bronx, he would indeed be subjected to such criticism.

The prescription is perverse not only because it misconceives the function of business. It is a breach of trust for a business to apply the funds entrusted to it to purposes other than those of business. Furthermore, a businessman is presumably qualified to conduct business. In itself that by no means gives him any special qualification to deal with social problems; nor is he appointed or elected to do so; nor, further, does he have to answer for his conduct to the people, as a politician who deals with social problems must do. Of course, those who demand that business shoulder this alleged social responsibility do not really want it to do so. They only want to be able to castigate it for its inevitable inability to do so.

However, the matter is not free from ambiguity. The business of a businessman is business. However, he is also a citizen, and as such he ought to do with his own funds and efforts whatever a good citizen should do. Furthermore, it may be proper to apply business funds to some social problems, as long as the purpose is a business one. Usually this philanthropy will be concerned with benefits to the locality where a business is situated, but it may extend to national affairs, such as, say, aid to private education, or to groups defending the integrity of the family or battling ideas subversive of the free economy, but all such contributions are made only on the footing that the true interests of business, in particular or in general, are thus protected or promoted. Thus, here again we may have a fuzzy borderline between proper and improper business behavior, but the principle should be clear in the businessman's mind. A corollary of the false social responsibility of business is the proposition that the pursuit of profit should not be the primary aim of business. Not infrequently one hears businessmen, especially among those who are styled as business leaders, endorse this proposition. They do not simply say that good business does not seek the fast buck but seeks profit through the lawful and honorable service of the consumer, which it would be right to say and say again. They declare that business has a higher purpose than the pursuit of profit, a notion which is false and which delivers business into the hands of those enemies who love to assert that profit itself is of dubious standing and that its pursuit is ignoble.

How do businessmen behave in ways which they think serve their interests but, in fact, undermine them? This is an old and familiar story. Every favor obtained by some business from the government at the expense of the consumer is a nail in the coffin of business, however avidly business seeks it and welcomes it. Protection against foreign imports is a familiar and long-standing example. Of course, it is always presented to the public as a policy or device to serve the general or national interest, but it is always inimical to the general interest (except in some theoretical cases, usually hypothesized by free-trade economists themselves who, however, have hastened to present cogent arguments for rejecting them in practice). Protection in practice always serves sectional interests only, and often even those only in the short run. Other governmental favors are of a like specious, harmful, and often counterproductive character. Nothing becomes business in a free society more ill than the way in which it maintains large lobbying staffs at the seats of government and rushes to the government for aid when it fails to pass the tests of the free market. Thereby it concedes to its collectivist enemies half their case against it. For if business needs to lean on the shoulders of government, why should not the government become the master of business? If business fails in its responsibility to serve the general interest, it almost invites the government to take over the reins of the economy, since the government par excellence presents itself to the public as the guardian of the general interest. To return to the issue of protection, we should note as a point of the highest importance that collectivism can never achieve ascendancy in a free-trade country without first removing freedom of foreign trade and erecting a protectionist wall around the country.

However, here again there are difficulties and ambiguities in practice. Lobbying for governmental favor is illegitimate and ultimately disastrous. Clean hands are a sine qua non for the lasting success and good health of business. But suppose that, as not infrequently happens, the government does, or proposes to do, something harmful to business. Then no doubt business has a right to lobby against it, but, of course, always on the footing that harm to freely competing, clean-handed business is harm to the people and their general interest, not simply to business. In practice there are cases where it is not easy to distinguish between justified resistance to harm threatened by the government and the quest for unjustified governmental favors from the government. But here again there is no difficulty in apprehending the principle, and in most cases in adhering to it. Witness the happy and admirable application of this principle to a substantially high degree in Britain from the mid-19th century to 1914.

Let us now turn to answering the critics and enemies of business by bolstering a defense which I have suggested is not as apt or well-considered as it needs to be. Consider, as a first example, the public attitude businessmen assume toward profits. Although the pursuit of profit is sometimes disclaimed as the prime end of business, businessmen do usually attempt to defend private profit. But how? All too often by demonstrating how small, even minuscule, it is as a return on capital or as a percentage of sales. Thus, for instance, they show that the oil companies' net profit per gallon of gasoline is a few cents and that the net profit of the most successful supermarket chains is less than 2 cents per customer's dollar. The figures are correct, but they do not disarm the collectivist. In his eyes private profit is illicit, however small. I have even heard distinguished businessmen defend profit on the basis that without profit to tax the government could not pay for its welfare activities, as if it were the function of business to finance the welfare state. Of course, they presented this defense because they know that their critics cherish the welfare state. This defense is actually surrender to the enemies of business. The correct defense is that the pursuit of profit is the spring and origin of abundance for the nation. It is the flywheel of the successful economy, and would be justified in a free economy whatever its magnitude. It costs the consumer less than nothing. It is, in fact, the consumer's Santa Claus, as is demonstrated by what he gets where profit is not pursued, as in the nationalized industries of the West, or where it is not allowed to be the economy's flywheel, as in the East.

Another common allegation is that the once-free economy has succumbed to the market power of Big Business. This, it is said, is the age of oligopoly. Hence, the economy is only part-free. Therefore, the state, which alone is properly to be invested with power, should assume the direction of the economy. The facts are otherwise, but business rarely presents them convincingly. The oligopolists, with their alleged market power, actually live in a whirlwind of competition. Yet, the critic may say, it is not price competition but competition only in styles, in appearances, in packaging and other frills. Untrue. In fact there is a raging wind of price competition among oligopolists. But to the extent that competition centers on other matters, it is the consumers themselves who so ordain. Not so, says the critic; it is the oligopolists whose advertising brainwashes the consumers into a desire for the frills.

If business really had the power to brainwash people into wanting what they would otherwise reject, it should have easily succeeded in instructing them in the true purposes and effects of advertising. In fact the consumer, who can change his purchasing patterns at any time, even in the case of durables, has a much stronger whip hand over the would-be persuader in the market than in the political arena when choosing among candidates for office or in the courtroom as a juror when weighing the persuasions of rival counsel. Yet in these cases people usually do not consider themselves to be brainwashed. In the market for goods the consumer is the real master, as every marketing professional soon discovers. Every day the consumers oblige the producers to pass examinations, and it is the consumers who allot the grades, not vice versa. The arts of persuasion serve essentially only to bring the producers' goods into the examination hall for the consumers' notice and scrutiny. They have very little power to induce the consumers to allot a passing grade day after day, test after test. The social value of advertising is, in fact, of a high order, and business has no reason to be timid or bashful in expounding it.

Now consider the campaign waged by Mr. Nader for nearly two decades supposedly against Big Business, but in fact against all business. From the beginning it was obvious to any instructed observer that the campaign was founded on a combination of ignorance and malice, to put it mildly, and the course of time has in no way mollified these features. Business had every possibility to expose the true character of the campaign. Yet its reaction was muted, timid, even almost respectful. It has paid dearly, and therefore the public has also paid dearly, for its failure to mount the vigorous defense which was needed. It is true that right from the beginning General Motors perceived the true character of Mr. Nader's campaign against the alleged faults of the Corvair, but unfortunately their method of dealing with him was so ill-considered that it proved to be sadly counterproductive.

Business needs the free society and the free society needs business. The enemies of business are also the enemies of the free society. The defects in business behavior to which I have drawn attention are not inherent in business. On the contrary, they run counter to the interests and successful conduct of business, and they sap its vitality. They can be corrected, and they will be when businessmen perceive how worthy of pride their role in society is, and also what power they can exert in the performance of that role.

The difference between the free and the unfree society resides in the functions of the state. In the free society the state is essentially limited to the protection of the freedom of the people. It fashions and maintains a framework of law within which and subject to which the citizens are free to make their own choices and go their own way. Under such a state, itself subject to the rule of law, business is the generator of the people's abundance, and it thus also enhances their freedom. Even more important it helps to breed a people of self-reliance and independence of spirit. With such a people the foundations of the state itself are fortified.

The collectivist state may set out to be the people's provider and benefactor, but it inevitably becomes their master. As it grows in scope and power, it conceives itself to be omnicompetent. From omnicompetence to omnipotence is a short step.

Business has a right and duty to oppose collectivism vigorously long before the stage of the omnipotent state is reached, indeed at its first signs and appearances. The obligation of business is to the people for the preservation of their prosperity, with which will go their freedom and their self-reliant and independent character. I have asserted that it is a breach of trust for business funds (as distinct from the private funds of businessmen as citizens) to be applied to nonbusiness purposes. But the preservation of the free society is also the preservation of business itself. Hence, it is a basic business purpose. It is a gross error to believe that in the disposition of its advertising funds, in the finance of its operations, or in its subventions to education, research, and enquiry, where they are proper, it must be neutral. That way lies the road to the Ford Foundation, the Rockefeller Foundation, and the Carnegie Endowment, which have become prime agents for the undermining of the system which produced the fortunes which endowed them. In eschewing a misconceived neutrality, business will fortify itself as well as the good of the people and, let it be said, enhance its own due and proper profitability. Notice in conclusion that it is proper and productive for business to forsake neutrality only when it ceases to be a sectional interest seeking the special favors of the state and truly becomes the champion and embodiment of the general interest. Until that time let it hide its ideological light under a bushel. But let us, the friends and well-wishers of business, help it to hasten the day when its light may rightly come out into the open.

Mr. Shenfield, former director of The British Industrial Policy Group and of The International Institute for Economic Research, is an economist, barrister, and author.

III.

THE CULTURAL SUBSTANCES OF FREEDOM

6.

Reopening the Books on Ethics: The Role of Education in a Free Society

John A. Howard

Edmund Burke, in his "Letter to the Sheriffs of the City of Bristol," addressed the central paradox of liberty, the inherent and never wholly reconcilable conflict between private judgment, which makes freedom a blessed estate, and the individual's responsibility to the community, which makes freedom a prickly burden. "The *extreme* of liberty," Burke asserted, "(which is its abstract perfection, but its real fault) obtains nowhere, nor ought to obtain anywhere. . . . Liberty must be limited to be possessed."[1]

The relentless tension between the human impulse to pursue one's own course and the necessity to modify one's conduct according to the needs of the group has challenged generations of philosophers and precipitated the collapse of powerful governments. This polarity must be dealt with in every organized endeavor—in commerce, industry, medicine, jurisprudence, and in the family. There is no immunity from it even for artistic creation, which by common consent demands for its fulfillment the utmost in independent judgment. Listen to the editors of the highly regarded *Saturday Review of Literature* in their denunciation of an award which the United States Library of Congress bestowed upon Ezra Pound for his *Pisan Cantos*:

> While one must divorce politics from art, it is quite another matter to use the word "politics" as a substitute for values. We do not believe, in short, that art has nothing to do with values. We do not believe that what a poet says is necessarily of lesser importance than the way he says it. We do not believe that a poet can shatter ethics and values and still be a good poet. We do not believe that poetry can convert words into maggots that eat at human dignity and still be good poetry.[2]

This editorial, I believe, speaks directly to the issue in question. The problem is certainly not how to prevent an Ezra Pound or anyone else from writing whatever seems important to him. The question, rather, is what shall the community prize and praise, what shall be the values and ideals and standards which shape the life of the society, and how shall worthy ideals and values be perpetuated. The editors of the *Saturday Review* were insisting that those who hold major responsibilities in the realm of public beliefs are inexcusably delinquent if they contribute to the destruction of standards of civilized conduct. The editors understood the importance of Burke's assertion that liberty must be limited to be possessed.

It has been 33 years since the *Saturday Review*'s criticism of the award committee created a heated controversy. During this last third of a century, there have been very few voices of intellectual or cultural prominence asserting and defending the interests of the entire society. In fact, this has been an era in which the parts have been granted virtually unquestioned dominance over the whole. The large debates have been about which of the competing interest groups shall prevail, not whether the common welfare would be served or injured by the outcome of an issue.

During the campus turmoil of the 1960s the statements, silences, actions, and inactions of the leaders of American colleges and universities illustrated and underscored this change away from a concern for the whole society to smaller parochial concerns. The open and sometimes violent assault by the student radicals upon the values and traditions and operating principles of the free society was of a much larger magnitude than the mere awarding of the literary prize to Mr. Pound. Almost no university president spoke out forcefully about the interests of the society which were then under attack. The *rational* public debate which did take place about the meaning and resolution of the campus convulsions seldom extended beyond a discussion of the nature and obligations of academic freedom. Academic freedom, to be sure, is a matter of basic importance, but one must ask: Is academic freedom more important than other principles of community life, more important than order, rationality and lawfulness?

When the campus turmoil had run its course, an altogether new set of assumptions had come to prevail in much of American higher education. One of those new principles seems to be that if academic freedom is not superior to all other considerations, at least no other public claims can be permitted to encroach upon the definition and application of academic freedom. Academic autonomy had been proclaimed. Although the ideas which crystallized in this new stance had been gaining support through many decades, the open assertion of the university's independence from the prevailing norms of the society marked a fundamental change from the concepts which had previously guided the course of American education.

The contrast between the old educational philosophy and the new one was brought into sharp focus by a report issued in 1979 by the Hastings Center in New York. In an analysis entitled "The Teaching of Ethics in the Undergraduate Curriculum 1876-1976," the author, Douglas Sloan, wrote:

> Throughout most of the nineteenth century the most important course in the college curriculum was moral philosophy, taught usually by the college president and required of all senior students. . . .
>
> The full significance and centrality of moral philosophy in the nineteenth-century college curriculum can only be understood in the light of the assumption held by American leaders that no nation could survive, let alone prosper, without some common moral and social values. . . .
>
> The entire college experience was meant above all to be an experience in character development and the moral life.[3]

Moral development was also the dominant concern in the schools as well as the colleges of that era. The McGuffey Readers, filled with little tales of moral elevation, were the common classroom sustenance of generations of Americans.

Let us consider briefly some of the factors which

contributed to the rejection of education's role as the guardian and tutor of public morals and ethics. One was the growing acceptance among faculty members of various new theories and philosophies, among them scientific naturalism, moral relativism, and subjectivity. More and more scholars had come to believe that the eternal verities had been proven false, or at least suspect, or were even barricades on the path to the total fulfillment of human nature. The rapidity with which ancient scientific certitudes yielded to new discoveries encouraged an analogy that ancient moral certitudes were equally vulnerable.

A second factor was a dramatic change in the qualifications of the people chosen as the leaders of American academic institutions. In the United States, prior to World War II, the college or university president characteristically took a major part in shaping the curriculum and guiding the educational program. Presidents Woodrow Wilson of Princeton, Robert Maynard Hutchins of Chicago, and James Bryan Conant of Harvard were not simply dynamic leaders of their universities, they were also commanding voices in the public discussion of educational philosophy. One is hard put to identify even one counterpart of those men today. In the last few decades the academic leaders seem to have been chosen for their skills in mediating conflicts, raising money, and managing complex organizations. The purposes of education languish in the councils of academic power; the agendas are almost totally devoted to the mechanics of financing and delivering education.

One other factor in the fundamental change in the concept of the relationship between education and society deserves comment. During the last forty years, the volume and cost of research conducted on the campuses has increased phenomenally. The salaries and the benefits now offered by universities in the competition to lure eminent research scholars to their premises have put the recruitment of renowned researchers almost on a par with that of professional football stars. In 1962, Harvard's President Pusey was moved to issue a formal report about the consequences of the massive research funds that had been flowing to the campuses from the government. Among other concerns, he noted that programs in science had grown rapidly in contrast to programs in all other fields of study and that the number of faculty appointments primarily devoted to research had grown out of all proportion to appointments for classroom teaching, which earlier had been the raison d'être of the university, so that decisions about many aspects of the university were affected by the large voting block of research-minded professors.

As the research function was catapulted into prominence, the principles which govern research activity tended to prevail in those instances where they were in conflict with the previous assumptions of the academic community. By its nature research must be uninhibited. It makes no sense to encourage a scholar to study a topic and tell him there are three aspects of it that are forbidden. All possibilities must be open to him if he is to perform his work thoroughly. By logical extension, it is judged inappropriate to impose limitations on the political, social, and even moral sympathies and affiliations of faculty members. From the research point of view, enthusiasts of violent revolution, partisans of sexual liberation, and advocates of any bizarre religious cult should be as eligible for a professorship as anyone else, provided they have the proper scholarly credentials. This research pressure against normative judgments reenforced the growing acceptance of moral relativism by the teaching faculty at a time when the academic leadership had already become little inclined to concern itself with such matters as the content and the character of the educational program and the impact that the educational program has upon the values, beliefs, and priorities of the students.

By the middle of the 1960s the faculty support for any normative stance on the part of the university had dwindled to the point that when the student militants made their demands, in many places the whole structure of policies and regulations through which traditional standards of conduct had been prescribed by the university was rapidly dismantled. On some campuses, the transformation not only involved the abdication of authority for all out-of-class aspects of the student's experience, but went so far as the sharing of authority with students for curricular planning, the performance rating of faculty members, the selection of the university president, and even membership on the Board of Trustees.

The consequences of this upheaval in the university's view of its relationship to the students can only be fully comprehended in the light of a clear understanding of the justification for the educational philosophy which had been abandoned. Douglas Sloan noted in the passage already cited that the American leaders of the 19th century believed that no nation could survive, let alone prosper, without common moral and social values. These earlier leaders perceived that the schooling in every country serves as the primary instrument by which the society imbues each new generation with a commitment to the ideals, the mores, and the institutions which characterize that particular kind of society and make it viable. It is not a question of simply imparting information about the *patria*, but rather of acculturating and indoctrinating the young as partisans of their homeland, carefully preparing them to accept and fulfill their responsibilities and obligations as citizens.

You will recognize this concept of a precise and demanding role for education was not an aberration that sprang up only in America, perhaps from puritanical New Englanders or from untutored frontiersmen. Rather, it was the American version of a long heritage of political and social theory deeply rooted in classical philosophy. During the 19th century, the United States was not alone in the prominence it gave to moral and ethical education. François Guizot, who successfully led the debate in the French Parliament to establish a national system of secondary education and then was named Minister of Education to implement that legislation, was above all a moralist. Earlier he had founded the first French pedagogical journal, *Les Annales de L'Éducation*, stressing in one editorial after another the necessity to imbue children with the principles of noble conduct.

Matthew Arnold, the English poet, but also an Oxford professor and for 35 years an inspector of British elementary schools, was chosen to head a delegation sent to France to try to discover why the French system of education seemed significantly more effective than the British one. Throughout that investigation, everywhere he went, Arnold encountered praise for Guizot and the priorities he had established. Matthew Arnold's own definition of education was "learning and propagating the best that has been thought and said in this world."

At the risk of belaboring the obvious, let us go to the next step and remind ourselves of the critical relationship between moral and ethical training and the well-being of the free society. For a nation as for every other group, be it family, athletic team, committee, or business enterprise, there must be some means by which the actions of the participants can be coordinated to achieve the objectives of the group. In the totalitarian society, decisions are made by the central authority as to what the citizens will do and will not do, and those decisions are enforced by terrorism, brainwashing, false imprisonment, and all the other techniques of tyranny. In the free society, the characteristic means of cooperation is the voluntary observance of informal codes of conduct. They include courtesy, honor, sportsmanship, lawfulness, integrity, professional ethics, marital fidelity, respect for private property, providing a good day's work for a good day's pay, and countless other informal norms.

The general observance of such standards of behavior contributes to an amicable and productive community. When people behave in a civilized fashion, it is easy to get along together. A large-scale rejection of these informal standards eats away at the fabric of good will and mutual trust which more than anything else makes life in the free society a friendly and agreeable circumstance in contrast to the state of permanent suspicion and fear which characterize the tyranny. If citizens increasingly disregard the informal civilized norms, all the systems and institutions of the society begin to operate less effectively; and when irresponsible conduct becomes widespread, the government is called on to pass more and more laws to regulate citizen behavior, so that the free society is converted into a system of government coercion. The breakdown of the informal codes of conduct is the precursor of the conversion of the free society to a controlled society.

Despite the flights of enthusiasm of philosophers and theorists asserting the contrary, history makes it clear that the human being, left to his own devices, is not likely to behave in a manner that promotes the well-being of the community. The definition of a savage is, after all, a person who does his own thing. Civilized behavior is learned behavior. We do ourselves a great disservice if we persist in believing the contrary. The apologists for the current non-normative stance of the universities insist that if students are exposed to various and contradictory views of mankind, and of the good society and the good life, their intelligence will lead them to wise or at least tolerable decisions about how they lead their own lives.

The response to that attitude of detached indifference about values was set forth by Gordon Chalmers in one of the very important works of educational philosophy to appear in the United States since 1950. Dr. Chalmers's book was entitled, significantly, *The Republic and the Person*. He wrote:

> The late William Allan Neilson, speaking at the 1940 Commencement of Kenyon College, told the graduates that his generation of university professors and presidents had been guilty of wrapping the young in romantic cotton wool. . . . Speaking of the aim and temper of college education, President Neilson quoted from *The City of Man* . . . the opinion of numerous intellectual leaders that the liberalism they had taught and promoted in the Twenties and Thirties was in important particulars established not on ethical fact, but on sentiment. It was, said the author of that volume, a "disintegrated liberalism." They stated that the illusions of the Thirties had produced a timidity and lack of conviction in many Americans concerning the true character of the Nazis and their threat to democracy. One may add that they also produced a romanticized notion of the true nature of Communism. This

sentimentalism was directly traceable to the ethical ignorance of persons thought to be learned. Many of these later admitted that the university world had persuaded the young that evil itself, extensive and malignant, does not exist.[4]

"The ethical ignorance of persons thought to be learned" is a hazard of no small consequences when it is prevalent in the academic community. Let us return again to the dominant non-normative orthodoxy of the universities. The process of education presupposes that knowledge has something to teach ignorance, experience something to teach inexperience, and informed judgment something to teach raw judgment. In the sciences, these suppositions still hold firm. The student is not subjected to a great range of conflicting views about gravity, genetics, and thermodynamics. He is provided with what is judged by the professor to be the most accurate and advanced understanding of the subject available. In science, a body of accumulated knowledge still has authority. However, in the more universally demanding realm of ethics and human values, ignorance, inexperience, and raw judgment have been proclaimed the equivalent of trained expertise. Each student is encouraged to arrive at his own conclusions. This is a rejection of the nature and the meaning of education, and one which the free society may not be able to withstand.

It is an easy thing to be critical of imperfect human beings and imperfect institutions. The more useful and more difficult role of the analyst is to offer some guidelines for better accomplishing the desired objectives. What we have asserted is a principle of the free society—the necessity for the educational system to prepare the young for responsible citizenship. The determination of what shall be the subject matter that attends to that principle is a complex and hazardous undertaking. There can be no single blueprint that serves all free societies equally well or even all communities in one society because, as Edmund Burke observed in the letter cited earlier, "social and civil freedom, like all other things in common life, are variously mixed and modified, enjoyed in very different degrees, and shaped into an infinite diversity of forms, according to the temper and circumstances of every community."[5]

The point of departure in designing a citizenship-training program needs to be the identification of principles of the free society that are vital to the community well-being. Let us touch on three illustrations that might qualify for that designation.

> 1. The principle of the rule of law. Each citizen needs to understand that chaos results when each person decides for himself which laws he will obey and which he will disregard. Each citizen must be brought to a recognition that the lawlessness of one individual harms all individuals. The ignorance of, or perhaps indifference to, this principle is approaching universality in the United States. There seems to be no recognition that when an individual takes up an illegal habit, for example the use of illegal drugs, the level of his concern for abiding by all other laws is automatically decreased.
>
> 2. The principle of orderly change. An enduring society must have provision for attending to new circumstances and new requirements. The free society does so through its legislative bodies at all levels of government. It is therefore important that the voters select as legislators individuals of integrity, objectivity, and breadth of understand-

ing who can accurately anticipate the probable consequences of the laws they enact, choosing a careful course that balances the proper interests of the citizens variously affected by the legislation. The degree to which this principle has faded from public consciousness in any free society can be measured by the character of the incumbent legislators. I must confess that integrity, objectivity, and broad knowledge do not come immediately to mind when one thinks of the members of the United States Congress. One hopes that other free nations are faring better in this regard.

3. The principles of justice. It is essential for the citizens to understand that the processes by which the free society mediates and adjudicates conflicts are dependent for their effectiveness on facts, objectivity, and rationality. When one party to an issue distorts the truth or asserts lies, or tries to stir up fear or hatred against the other party, not only is the just resolution of the conflict jeopardized, but a process of the utmost importance to the free society is compromised. We are now seeing the institutionalization of the antithesis of this principle in the argumentation of public issues. Emotions and partial truths tend to dominate in the argumentation of difficult questions, the nuclear freeze being a current example.

It will be recognized that each civic principle identifies a pattern of behavior which must prevail and therefore must be instilled in the hearts and minds of the citizens, the three principles we have cited pointing variously to the necessity for lawfulness, truthfulness, a respect for the rights of others, and the intelligent fulfillment of one's voting privilege. Moral education is the automatic partner of and the necessary complement to citizenship education. While there will be some principles on which curriculum planners may readily reach an agreement, the difficult part of arriving at a full agenda for civic and moral education is how to deal with subjects on which there is strong disagreement. In this respect, the experience of the United States offers guidance.

Until quite recently in America, the primary authority for the governance of education was decentralized. It was the responsibility of each local school board and each board of trustees of a college or university to determine the educational purposes and priorities that would prevail in the program under its jurisdiction. The benefits of decentralized control were many and substantial. In the first place, there was a wholesome diversity of policies, programs, and techniques which not only well served the pluralistic nature of the nation, but also led to wide experimentation in the improvement of educational programs. In the second place, a great many citizens, and especially the parents of students, were able to involve themselves in the deliberations about the educational program because they had direct access to the people of their own community who controlled the policy decisions of the schools. Furthermore, if the decisions made by the school policymakers did not satisfy the people, they could take action to elect different policymakers. Those who governed the educational program had to be responsible to the parents of the students. And finally, when the primary determinant in educational policies is the central government, as is now the case in the United States, any effort to address such matters as moral and civic education is reduced to the lowest common denominator of agreement. And in the present state of our culture, that

Reopening the Books on Ethics

means virtual oblivion. One is inclined to believe that what is gained by the decentralization of educational responsibility is greater than what is lost through an absence of national standards and uniform priorities.

Well, what have we said here? First, that every free society must find ways to deal with the conflict between the desires of the individual and the obligations he must accept as a member of the community. Second, that the process of formal schooling is the mechanism by which the society assures that the common interests are protected and this is done by training the young people to understand their own nation, to adopt its ideals, and to abide by its requirements. Third, that one of the absolutely fundamental requirements of the free society is the acceptance by the citizens of many informal codes of conduct, those standards of behavior constituting the means by which the free society addresses that tension between the individual and the group. Fourth, that whereas the schools and colleges in the United States and some other nations formerly transmitted the ideals and the informal codes of conduct quite effectively through granting a high priority to character education and citizenship education, that activity has largely been discontinued. One observer has phrased this change as a shift from education to learning. And here, I wish to pick up a loose end. In mentioning the conflict between the principles governing research and those governing education, I should have observed that there is no reason why those two functions cannot be conducted on the same premises with productive interaction so long as the distinguishing principles of each are recognized and appropriately safeguarded. Fifth, we have commented upon the processes of determining what should comprise the agenda of character education and citizenship education, with the principles of the free society constituting the absolute base for that determination.

The educational system has largely disassociated itself from one of its functions, a function that is critically important to the strength and survival of a free society. We have, in the United States, produced several generations of cultural orphans, people who have little knowledge and even less appreciation of their heritage of freedom, or the struggles and sacrifices which produced it. By failing to impart to our citizens a passionate devotion to their freedom and an understanding of their obligations as free citizens, we have inadvertently engaged in a kind of unilateral intellectual disarmament which could well prove more devastating to the cause of liberty than would the voluntary destruction of our defense arsenals.

I suggest that there is no task of such importance for the schools and colleges, and few tasks of such importance for free governments, as the reconstitution of effective programs of moral and civic education.

Notes

[1] Edmund Burke, Published Letter, May 16, 1977, cited in Peter J. Stanlis, ed., *Edmund Burke, On Conciliation With The Colonies and Other Papers* (Lunenberg, Vermont: The Stinebour Press, 1975), p. 255.

[2] *Saturday Review of Literature*, "A Reply to Mr. Evans," July 2, 1949, 32:22, cited in Gordon Keith Chalmers, *The Republic and the Person* (Chicago: Henry Regnery Company, 1952), p. 25.

[3] Douglas Sloan, "The Teaching of Ethics in the American Undergraduate Curriculum 1876-1976", Hastings Center Report (Hastings-on-Hudson, New York, December 1979), pp. 21-23.

[4] Chalmers, op. cit., pp. 3, 4.

[5] Burke, idem.

Dr. Howard, president of The Rockford Institute, is the former president of the American Association of Presidents of Independent Colleges and Universities and is coauthor of *Who Should Run the University?* and *Dilemmas Facing the Nation*.

7.

Feeling Unfree: Freedom and Fulfillment in Contemporary Culture

Ronald Berman

My first impulse in addressing the topic of freedom and contemporary culture is to enumerate the ways in which the realm of literate mass culture—of magazines and movies, quiz shows and novels, advertisements and Sunday supplements—disregards freedom. It is understandable that freedom should there be disregarded because that realm is so largely devoted to the values of entertainment, as are even newspapers and the 6 o'clock news, which, one hopes, is morally deflationary. And yet, wherever contemporary culture is literate it is didactic, even opinionated: we get astonishing amounts of advice on how to live and think from talk shows, from columnists and celebrities who have become savants; from public-interest advertising and from just plain commercials; from bumper stickers and from the counseling that obscures the light everywhere. We hear about values continually that have a much higher specific gravity than the forms conveying them, itself a major rhetorical problem.

It turns out that even though contemporary culture wants to entertain us or to express itself or to get us to buy something, it has quite an appetite for ideas. Freedom is not generally one of these ideas, unless it is the freedom to make a marketplace choice. We hear most often in movies and on television about other themes: satisfaction, security, equality, pleasure. Let me reserve this for a moment and go on to a related subject: not the way in which freedom is disregarded but the way in which it is devalued.

Much of what we read or hear insists that democracy prospers because it is selfish and that it has no other claim on our allegiance than prosperity. This attitude is sometimes fostered by free enterprise. It is always a re-education to return to Schumpeter, to read about "the extent to which the bourgeoisie, besides educating its own enemies, allows itself in turn to be educated by them. It absorbs the slogans of current radicalism and seems quite willing to undergo a process of conversion to a creed hostile to its very existence."[1] This was written before the '60s. To bring it up to date, here is Irving Kristol's account of marketing and ideas:

> Liberal capitalism doesn't see nihilism as an enemy, but rather as just another splendid business opportunity.
>
> One of the most extraordinary features of our civilization today is the way in which the "counterculture" of the New Left is being received and sanctioned as a "modern" culture appropriate to "modern" bourgeois society. Large corporations today happily publish books and

magazines, or press and sell records, or make and distribute movies, or sponsor television shows which celebrate pornography, denounce the institution of the family, revile the "ethics of acquisitiveness," justify civil insurrection, and generally argue in favor of the expropriation of private industry.[2]

In short, we are willing enough ourselves to dissociate economic and political freedom. And so are others. When we do hear of freedom in the realm of mass culture it is often to learn that our culture is insufficiently free. I take it to be the standard educated view that American society is affluent but unhappy and that because of this it needs a kind of change not provided by ordinary and constitutional methods.

I have used the word "unhappy" with some forethought, and I take this "unhappiness" and its relationship to freedom as one of my primary themes. Unhappiness with ourselves and with the way things are comprises more than disillusion, more even than what Thomas Hardy called "the ache of modernism." Perhaps I should say it comprises *less* than that, for I am speaking of literal unhappiness, of dissatisfaction with the rewards of social life—and of dissatisfaction with the role of government in purveying those rewards. It is everywhere assumed that political freedom is a good thing but that it means less than we think. Neither political freedom nor economic freedom leads, the critics of industrial democracy say, to other and more necessary things: among them authentic personal freedom. One assumption of the Marxian critique of life in the industrial West, a critique diffused everywhere some person or association has a quarrel with life, is that political freedom means little of itself. It has not, after all, made us happy.

In fact, the West has caused our unhappiness by endowing us with the consequences of free choice—free choice in matters humanly irrelevant. The more material goods we consume, according to Marcuse and many others, the more opiated we become by meaningless alternatives. And the less healthy and happy we are. The observation that democratic society is in some ways neurotic is not original. As on so many other things, Tocqueville seems to have gotten there first. He wrote in *Democracy in America* that there seemed to be a kind of principle of diminishing emotional returns in democratic life:

> The more equal men are, the more insatiable will be their longing for equality.
>
> Among democratic peoples men easily obtain a certain equality, but they will never get the sort of equality they long for. That is a quality which ever retreats before them without getting quite out of sight, and as it retreats it beckons them on to pursue. Every instant they think they will catch it, and each time it slips through their fingers. They see it close enough to know its charms, but they do not get near enough to enjoy it, and they will be dead before they have fully relished its delights.
>
> That is the reason for the strange melancholy often haunting inhabitants of democracies in the midst of abundance, and of that disgust with life sometimes gripping them in calm and easy circumstances.[3]

This is an entirely remarkable passage, and not

only because of its psychological insight. That phrase about the strange melancholy haunting democracy suggests the tragic view of life, a view which today has little to commend it but its truth. But for our present purpose it is sufficient to note that Tocqueville accepts the proposition that in the midst of freedom there is never equality; in the midst of abundance there will be disgust.

There is a large modern audience which would prefer to hear not that satisfaction always diminishes but that the state should change conditions so that satisfaction will be perfect. And I mean by this the full range of satisfaction, from the consumption of goods to the erotic or spiritual condition. Marcuse touched a nerve of this audience when he wrote in *One-Dimensional Man* that a society which denies authentic satisfaction is not legitimate. He had in mind needs rather than rights, a distinction which alters traditional political discussion. So far as needs are concerned, he wrote, there are in the media so many images of appetites gratified, so many suggestions of emotional and sensory plenitude that we mistakenly believe our most natural desires are fulfilled. But for him and for his constituency the illusion of happiness—which is the recognition of satisfaction—is the grand illusion of our society.

One acknowledges that from Aristotle on there has been an important existential component to political theory. The *Politics* repeatedly states that we have an obligation to foster the "spirit" of individuals. It adds that the just government will respect human association and that it will promote trust and even confidence in its citizens. But with the accelerated political developments of modern times some new variables have been added to the conception of state responsibility. Right now, the state is viewed by many who read, write, or take treatment as the natural recourse for unhappiness. It is responsible not only for the objective conferral of freedom but for the subjective response to that freedom. We are now not alone entitled to the pursuit of happiness, but to its actual capture.

The argument that we are essentially unfree has proceeded since the second rise of radicalism in the sixties. It is now embedded in a variety of fields and vocations: in economics, communications, literary criticism, aesthetics, and especially in the burgeoning vocations of self-help and self-fulfillment. There are more books on assertiveness training in a typical bookstore, even a typical university bookstore, than there are on Shakespeare, Milton and Dante combined.

It is possible to argue in the new economics that free enterprise is fraudulent because it does not lead to the personal consciousness of satisfaction. There is freedom, but that is confined only to entrepreneurs. The rest are involuntary consumers of goods and services which are peddled irresistibly by advertising. The idea is familiar not only to the reader of Marcuse but, more in the mainstream, to the reader of Galbraith as well.

There are, I think, two points to the psychic attack on enterprise: first, that economic freedom disguises political tyranny and second, that authentic needs (which we now understand to be full-fledged rights) are not served by the marketplace. Here is what a second-generation Marcusian economist has to say about the meaning of "truly human needs." They are as follows: "Meaningful participation in sexual intercourse, a sense of belonging to a human community, a feeling of potency and participation in the determination of one's destiny, and a sense of purpose and creativity."[4]

Here is a wonderful confusion between potency and power. But we can see at any rate how the grounds of discourse have shifted. When political and economic freedom work, there is little left to do but attack their success—or their limits. One of the important things about the passage just cited is its assertion of subjective over objective. It does not state that creativity leads to creation. We are not being asked the fairly sensible question of distinguishing between various kinds of actual value. What we are being asked is whether freedom makes us happy—or potent.

Another second-generation Marcusian, in communications, describes contemporary culture in the democratic West as a failure because people within it *feel* unfree. And he describes that culture as characterized by "frustration," "futility," and "social entrapments."[5] These are useful phrases to the observer, because they plainly imply that political and economic freedom does not liberate men from their own mentalities. The idea of unfreedom has undergone a translation: it now refers not to the exercise of political rights but to the way we feel about the choices we have made. Nowhere has this become more plain than in the advice industry. The postwar period may become for the future historian the Age of Counseling, with some of the main subjects for historical analysis being abortion, alcohol, diet, employment, happiness, health, personality, and sexual relationships. There are now counselors of every kind attached to most institutions, and therapy has become a way of life. A certain amount of this has infiltrated education: not only is counseling proffered on race and sex but credit is given for almost every kind of course whose object is to produce some material change in the enrolled student. Perhaps that puts it too abstractly. It might be said that intelligence is not an end of such courses, nor is vocational skill, nor is the transmission of a body of knowledge. The course is conceived of as a corrective to an imperfect social system.

According to several useful formulations this is an age of analysis. But it is useful to see in what ways analysis has become political when it becomes social. In one of Lionel Trilling's last books there is a splendid treatment of democratic repressiveness: of the idea that freedom results in something a good deal worse than melancholy or unhappiness. Trilling wrote of R. D. Laing's work on schizophrenia as if it were (as it seems to be) a form of political theory on tyranny.[6] He took seriously Laing's statement that mental illness is caused by "society through the agency of the family." Schizophrenia is, according to Laing, one consequence of cultural unfreedom, occurring when patients unable to resolve the obviously false demands of society with their innocent perception of the way things should be become passive and silently withdraw into themselves. That is to say, because they are coerced into unsatisfying jobs or relationships or made to accept normative ideas or turned by the uncaring state over to the repressive care of family and other institutions, they exemplify literally the sickness of the West.

Perhaps even more interesting than the thought of leftists on therapeutic politics is that of those nearer the center of the spectrum. Our subject has been considered by Rollo May who, in the recent book *Freedom and Destiny*, illustrates the quarrel that mental-health liberalism has with political liberty. The book is remarkably central to our purpose, for it is a conscious attempt to redefine freedom by purging it of those things which the Higher Therapy finds offensive. We begin with the recognition that freedom is part of a past we have outgrown: it is associated with the kind of primitivism, moral and emotional, displayed by the

Feeling Unfree

right and long since given up by the left. Such is my interpretation of the book's beginning, which says,

> The flagrant denial of personal freedom can be seen in precisely the shrillest and loudest protestations of *protecting* our freedom. One need only glance back at the McCarthys, the Dieses, and the Jenners. . . . Such hypocrisy has become almost identified with the use of the word "freedom" in the minds and hearts of many people. When a high-school commencement speaker or a Fourth of July orator harangues us with phrases like "America, land of the free," we yawn and look up vaguely to see how he, in the pattern set by McCarthy, proposes to hoodwink us.[7]

There are a good many things happening in this passage: it expresses a sense of present against past, of national civilization against regional backwardness, and, most important, of freedom as personal rather than traditionally political. And indeed May dislikes the idea that political procedures can really illuminate the idea of freedom: he goes from civic to national backwardness in his description of the 1980 elections: "In the speeches at the political conventions in the summer of 1980, it was notable that the more conservative and reactionary the speaker, the more he tended to use the term 'freedom.'" (pp. 12-13)

We all know with Samuel Johnson that patriotism is the last refuge of a scoundrel, but May's argument tries to establish something extra. It suggests that traditional ideas about freedom—and freedom itself—will not do for the modern world. It argues, as mainstream liberalism often does, for the exigencies of the moment. And it suggests that political freedom does not provide social health. A healthy society is not to be judged by its performance but by its essence. One does not view it vis-à-vis voting rights or electoral choice. A healthy society is psychologically and morally free; it does not go to war; it does not suffer from inflation or unemployment or from mass unhappiness. If it should exhibit those things it would be illegitimate (cf. May, p. 19). In an unhealthy and illegitimate society, the one we now have, the role of the political therapist is to make us aware of how society should be changed. Within that context, his central purpose is to concentrate attention on the problem of personal rather than political freedom. For it is personal freedom, or rather the consciousness of it, that validates citizenship. We see in the following statement by May the redefinition of freedom as an individual and not a social concept, a psychological and not a political condition:

> When a person loses his freedom, there develops in him an apathy, as in the blacks in slavery, or neurosis or psychosis as in twentieth-century people. . . . we can define neurosis and psychosis as lack of communicativeness, "shut-up-ness," inability to participate in the feelings and thoughts of others or to share oneself with others. Thus, blind to his own destiny, the person's freedom is also truncated. (pp. 20-21)

This is grammatically, syntactically, philosophically a mess but it is what a lot of people now are thinking. What May and others object to, of course, is the nature not of freedom but of human relationships: they never ask whether those with feelings to communicate deserve to be heard. And the honorific idea of "participation," one of the great vulgarisms of the age, serves to legitimate the individual will by suggesting its multiplied otherness. If we are interested in freedom in contemporary culture we ought to recognize the change in definition. According to the politics of mental health, the social and political conditions we live under cause neurosis. Neurosis is to be known by unhappiness. Unhappiness reflects directly on that political freedom under which it transpires. Political freedom is therefore in opposition to personal freedom. This last accounts for several mysteries of cultural politics. The first such mystery concerns our extraordinary hospitality toward totalitarian idealism. As has been widely noted, pilgrims from the West give their most enthusiastic and unqualified praise to the spirit of Soviet or Chinese society. They do this while readily admitting that actual daily life is repressive. But they admire the tranquilized character of those under communist rule, especially their freedom from doubt. This is less naive than is generally thought. The pilgrims know about censorship and the one-party state and the secret police. But they prefer them, at least for other people, to the political ambiguities of freedom. A decade ago Norman Mailer found that Cubans were happy—or that he was happy at the thought of happy Cubans. Today the same applies to the sympathetic visitor to Vietnam or the Soviet Union. It is not that such visitors are unaware of tyranny, but that they believe there are more important things than freedom for mental health.

The second mystery of cultural politics has been illuminated in a recent article by Richard Grenier in *Commentary*. He writes that:

> In recent times the structure and institutions of society have come to be held responsible, not only for social and racial justice, the pattern of distribution of wealth, and economic misery and

deprivation, but for the highly personal problems of the individual. In this new style of thought, the individual is seen to be less and less responsible for his own happiness. If he does not attain personal fulfillment and self-realization, it is the fault of "society." Examining statements by young Americans who joined the Venceremos Brigade in Cuba, [Paul] Hollander observes [in the *American Sociologist*] that it is hard to imagine Robespierre, Bakunin, Lenin, or Trotsky voicing such sentiments as the following: "I am all f[—] up. Too many problems that I have to deal with. I am amazingly selfish . . . that's certainly how we are taught in a capitalist society, and I am a child of capitalism." Or, "I am beginning to understand how very thin is the line between neurosis and oppression."[8]

Grenier's article is on movies, the great source of images and self-images for the half-educated of the West. In it he suggests that the restlessness, apathy, anomie, alienation, unhappiness, self-contempt, libidinal and actual impotence—and I suppose we should add "melancholy"—which are such large themes of contemporary film are associated with what Rainer Fassbinder called *das System*. Fassbinder did not mean East Germany. He meant the source of all psychic unhappiness and disorder: the culture of the West under which freedom has wrecked the libido. It is no wonder that potency and power have been confused.

As Christopher Lasch sees the matter, there is in fact a "sickness" of modern times. But it comes from the doctrine of fulfillment itself: "the more the 'liberated' man clamors for fulfillment, the more he succumbs to hypochondria, to melancholy, or to a suicidal self-hatred that alternates, not with occasional heights of rapture, but with a chronic mild depression, the dominant mood of the times."[9] We come back to Tocqueville after all, with the same phrase being used to describe a related condition.

Contemporary culture is very large, and I have been looking over a very small part of it: the diagnostic attempts of critics on the left to devalue freedom. As the Venceremos Brigade member observed, there is indeed a fine line betweeen neurosis and oppression. But the critics of freedom are given enough ammunition. This is a contemporary culture, after all, in which we hear that "Freedom's waiting for you" at 7/11 convenience stores; in which the phrase "living free" refers to deodorants; in which the conception of liberty means (in terms synchronous with parlor Marxism) personal satisfaction. The more that freedom is seen this way the more a kind of Gresham's Law of language will obtain. After enough years of being assured that freedom is an aspect of consumption, after constantly being assured by those one step of consciousness ahead of the mass that freedom is a form of self-satisfaction, the general understanding may well be confused.

Contemporary culture has encouraged us to believe that if we are not happy we are oppressed. Many people accept that idea. In so doing they have moved from objective and political reasoning to subjective and psychological awareness. One major problem this causes is the problem of consistency, a problem of what one might call the problem of the conservation of meaning. The criteria of satisfaction are so personal, so deeply connected to the mysteries of pleasure, even to those of sexual satisfaction, that a common language may be hard to find. The woman who feels unfree because the atmosphere of history is masculine and the man who feels unfree because he is either powerless or not potent may not have treatable complaints.

But they certainly do have philosophical complaints. In his splendid book *The Liberal Mind*, Kenneth Minogue observed that anxiety over mental health was connected to the belief that human conflict is irrational and ought not to be endured. If there is troublesome economic competition between corporations they must learn to cooperate and the problem must be dissolved. If there are disparities of wealth which cause envy then the disparities rather than the envy must be abolished. In short, to quote Minogue, "modern doctrine scientifically sees friction between individuals as the result of neurosis, aggression, and frustration" and has decided, finally, that "it has found a cure for those, too."[10]

There is probably nothing more central to our purpose than those passages in Freud's *Civilization and Its Discontents* which deal with the limits of satisfaction. The great problem is, he said, that "we are threatened with suffering from three directions: from our own body, which is doomed to decay and dissolution and which cannot even do without pain and anxiety as warning signals; from the external world, which may rage against us with overwhelming and merciless forces of destruction; and finally from our relations to other men." There are two solutions—to put up with this, so that the pleasure principle becomes the reality principle—or to regard reality "as the sole enemy and as the source of all suffering, with which it is impossible to live, so that one must break off all relations with it."[11] The implementation of the second solution, Freud says, causes one to re-create the world, and it is of enormous interest that he speaks here not only of madness but of the institutional organization of our fears into religious and demireligious doctrines.

The new mass psychology—now at home in television and in movies, in place on all commercial bookshelves, believed in by all who have a quarrel with the way things are—has decided to re-create reality. It has learned what perfect social health ought to be, and is hostile to whatever inhibits that. It is not only then that institutions or standards are opposed as barriers to cathexis, but that whatever gives society its organizing idea is also opposed. A free society is too full of ambiguities, is too disordered to allow the free play of the individual will: that will comes up against too many conflicts which are natural to the condition of freedom. At any rate, freedom implies failure just as it implies success and it is much more psycho-politically useful to believe that the world is wrong than that failure is inevitable.

It is not entirely correct to believe that the democracies of the West are fearful of the cost of responsibility. They have come to believe what they have been often told. They have been lectured for years on the primacy of the individual will and on the transcendent value of fulfilling desires. They have identified these desires as needs, and these needs as rights. They have been assured by the Higher Therapy that a social order is only legitimate when it fulfills those desires-needs-rights, and that an infallible way of detecting that is to query one's own consciousness of satisfaction. So it is not then entirely that the West fears the power of the Soviet Union as a threat to life; it fears that the principle of diminishing returns may be true. Especially for those who have risen into the middle class recently, it is intolerable to find that with mobility and prosperity it is still possible to be unhappy. They ask of government what many now expect of it, that it should make them free in a sense somewhat different from that anticipated by this discussion.

They naturally want government either to get on with the main job of life as perceived by so much of the demiphilosophy of our time, which is to change the human condition, or else to admit that it has no claim on them. It is tempting to use a term which has been often invoked—the *failure of nerve*—to explain much that has transpired from the collapse of classical religion to the decline of modern education to the present circumstance of indifference to political freedom. But I think it might be better to presume some assertion of ideas. For a long time the religious enthusiasms and philosophical utopias of the West have celebrated emotional primacy. And there has been since the 18th century a well-established conviction that individual happiness stands in opposition to social order. We have added some new ingredients: among them the rejection of the idea of emotional conflict and the acceptance of the idea that the state is custodian of personal happiness. Almost without notice we have changed certain conceptions, among them that of freedom.

Freedom in the political sense alone seems not to carry much of a psychological payload. Societies governed by it seem to hostile curiosity to have gone on only to more prosperous inequality, not to have approached the satisfaction of our truest needs and most fundamental, emotional rights. If the aim is for the individual to *feel* free rather than to *be* free then there is no need to keep up obsolete reverence, to believe in, even to allegorize liberty. I don't find the West today to be as nihilistic as is sometimes suggested. But it is obsessed with the articulation of feeling and with the attainment of tranquility. Nirvana is not really possible but it is promised by movies, pulps, advertisements, therapy, and propaganda. Even a non-idea may have a time that is come. Especially a non-idea which is so marvelously wrapped in morality and self-consciousness and which accuses freedom rightly of something to which it has always been vulnerable, that it can never be extensive enough. There is a wonderful line from *As You Like It* which I will misapply to my conclusion: "I can live no longer by thinking." A great many people want to think no more. And that too means something for freedom.

Notes

[1] Joseph Schumpeter, *Capitalism, Socialism and Democracy* (New York: Harper & Row, 1975), p. 161.

[2] Irving Kristol, "Capitalism, Socialism, and Nihilism," *Two Cheers for Capitalism* (New York: Basic Books, 1978), pp. 66-67.

[3] Alexis de Tocqueville, "Why the Americans Are Often So Restless in the Midst of Their Prosperity," *Democracy in America*, eds. J.P. Meyer and A.P. Kerr (New York: Doubleday, 1969), 538.

[4] J.Ron Stanfield, *Economic Thought and Social Change* (Carbondale, Illinois: Southern Illinois University Press, 1979), p. 67.

[5] These terms have been quoted from Stuart Ewen, *Captains of Consciousness* (New York: McGraw-Hill, 1976).

[6] Lionel Trilling, *Sincerity and Authenticity* (New York: Harcourt Brace Jovanovich, 1973), pp. 159-161.

[7] Rollo May, *Freedom and Destiny* (New York: W.W. Norton & Co., 1981), p. 12. Hereafter cited parenthetically.

[8] Richard Grenier, "Fassbinder & The Bloomingdale's Factor," *Commentary*, 74 (October 1982), 59.

[9] Christopher Lasch, *Haven in a Heartless World* (New York: Basic Books, 1979), p. 183.

[10] Kenneth Minogue, *The Liberal Mind* (New York: Random House, 1968), p. 87.

[11] Sigmund Freud, *Civilization and Its Discontents* (New York: W. W. Norton & Co., 1961), pp. 24, 28.

Dr. Berman, professor of Renaissance Literature at the University of California—San Diego, is the author of *America in the Sixties: An Intellectual History* and of several works of literary criticism.

8.

New Hymns for the Republic: The Religious Right and America's Moral Purpose

Richard John Neuhaus

The theme under consideration, "For Your Freedom, and Ours," suggests that freedom is indivisible. There is an important measure of truth in that assumption. I am constrained to remember, however, that the forms of freedom's expression and the structure essential to its protection are various. A shared commitment to freedom must be accompanied by respect for the diversity of national and cultural interests and sensibilities.

Americans have not always shown such respect. In the period since World War II, the U.S. *imperium* has frequently been tied to the false and arrogant assumption that we Americans are the sole exemplars and teachers, appointed to instruct the world in the meaning of democratic freedom. This is an endemic flaw in America's understanding of its role in the world. Long before World War II—indeed virulently in the time before World War I, when America thought itself untainted by the ambiguities of world power—the idea of "the American exception" to the tyrannical nature of world history was deeply rooted in our self-consciousness as a people. Truth to tell, the notion of "the American exception" is implicit and explicit in the documents of our founding as a nation. As almost all historians agree, that notion was grounded in religion. More specifically, it was grounded in perceived analogies between the American experience and the experience of Israel of old. We declared ourselves the "New Israel" and a "light upon the hill"; we were not only an audacious experiment in freedom but the product of divine intervention portending the democratic freedom of all humankind.

G.K. Chesterton's observation that "America is a nation with the soul of a church" touches upon a truth that continues to puzzle and infuriate friends and foes alike. There is a vast British, Continental, and American literature devoted to the lament that America seems incapable of the "maturity" required for the exercise of power within the accepted terms of what Hans Morgenthau calls "politics among nations." Yet it may also be that this "immaturity" is necessarily related to the vitalities of America's domestic life and role in the world. Unlike most other historic powers, America is not a nation by demographic and geographical accident, nor demarcated by the force of arms. America is a people on purpose and by purpose. America is self-consciously an invention, in need of regular renewal by re-invention. It is an idea restlessly in search of, and always falling short of, secure embodiment. And the central idea animating the search is that of freedom.

This may seem to be a romantic view of the American experience. And it would be romantic, to be sure, were we to ignore the economic, geopolitical, and military factors that have shaped and continue to shape America. Yet I believe it remains the case that most Americans believe that America is, above all, an idea. Even those who excoriate the "bourgeois myth" of freedom agree that that is indeed what constitutes the American myth. Between those who believe freedom is the truth to be advanced and those who believe it is the myth to be debunked, there is no dispute that it is freedom that is at issue. There is also a curious agreement that, among the nations, America is somehow the key actor in the unfolding of universal history. On this point there has not been much change during the last two centuries. The dramatic new debate is over whether America is the key actor for good or for evil. A century ago it was routinely asserted that America is the chief source of the hope for universal freedom and felicity. Today among some Americans it is as routinely asserted that America, and its influence in the world, is the chief obstacle to universal liberation and equality. To sober observers, both views cannot help but seem exaggerated.

American self-understanding seems to lurch from hubris to self-debasement, from illusions of omnipotence to groveling for the status of impotence, from believing that it is too good for the sordid world to believing the world must be saved from its sordid self. But whether in self-congratulation or in self-flagellation, always there is this moral, even moralistic tone. The notion of "national character" has been subjected to severe criticism in recent decades, but it must nonetheless be said that it is peculiarly the national character of America that is in question. The sustained reinvention and reassertion of moral purpose is perhaps necessary in the absence of any other national character. We all think we have some grip on what it means to be a Frenchman, a German, a Spaniard, or an Englishman. But what is an American apart from this sense of moral purpose? As the apparent cacophony of American pluralism becomes more evident with the decline of the White-Anglo-Saxon-Protestant hegemony, the statement of moral purpose becomes more urgent rather than less.

Americans need an excuse for *being*, especially for being so very big and so very blessed. Without such an excuse, our unseemly impingement upon world history is an unbearable embarrassment. American leaders have regularly articulated America's sense of singular, even providential, moral purpose. The statements of the Founding Fathers are well known, and are today both parodied as pretentious and reverently recalled in an effort to "turn America around" to its constituting vision. Those who parody the pretentiousness of it all are usually called liberal, while those who would revitalize the founders' sense of radical historical experiment are, strangely enough, called conservative. Beyond the Founding Fathers, there were Lincoln's musings on America as "the last best hope of man on earth." In this century, Woodrow Wilson is variously scorned or cheered for expressing a similar intuition regarding the American mission. But almost every presidential administration has felt called upon to engage itself in national missiology. One thinks of Roosevelt's "four freedoms," or more recently, Carter's mission with regard to human rights, or today, Reagan's uncertain trumpet-calling for a "crusade for democracy."

Is this perennial restatement of an American

mission a sign of immaturity? Perhaps so. But it can be persuasively argued that America is on mission by necessity. Reductionist economic and geopolitical explanations of the American phenomenon offer no coherent or politically empowering self-understanding of America. In addition, the general sociological theories which explain the basis of moral legitimacy in the founding of other cities and nations are of very limited use when applied to America. That is, the theory that societies are founded upon family gods—upon the sacred associations surrounding *gentes*, phratries, and tribes—fails in the absence of founding families in America. To be sure, there are partisans of patrician legitimation in America, such as the Daughters of the American Revolution and others who boast of family lineage from the 17th century. But such vaunting of legitimating lineage is on the decline and has always been suspect as antidemocratic. The moral legitimation of America continues to be premised upon the sentiment inscribed on every dollar bill, "*Novus Ordo Seclorum,*" a new order for the ages.

And despite the constitutional disestablishment of religion, American moral legitimation is closely related, as a tree is related to its roots, to a theological legitimation. In official assertion and popular sentiment, America is an experiment for providential purpose. And again, that purpose is most characteristically associated with exemplifying and advancing democratic freedom. This is the belief undergirding Woodrow Wilson's notion of the conflict that had as its aim to "make the world safe for democracy." It is a measure of the legitimation crisis in American life today that many opinion leaders, including many in the churches, declare that America's idea of democracy is not safe for the world.

It may be misleading to speak of "America's idea

of democracy," since among Americans there are different and sometimes conflicting ideas of democracy. Indeed, as is well known, the attractions of democratic rhetoric are such today that even totalitarian societies make a point of styling themselves as democratic. The historical sources of democratic thought are various; there are classical, French, and several English versions of democracy. The constitutional effort in America was self-consciously drawing upon and modifying these sources, both past and contemporary. That effort probably reached its greatest doctrinal clarity in the *Federalist Papers* written by Madison, Hamilton and Jay. One point on which they, especially Madison, were very clear is that absolute doctrinal clarity is neither possible nor desirable, especially with respect to the transcendent or religious legitimations of democracy.

In the view of most students, this deliberate unclarity has been a source both of vitality and confusion in American history. The confusion is evident today in the way that those who style themselves as "liberals" invoke the constituting vision to legitimate both extreme libertarianism and statist control aimed at advancing "democratic equality." Both democratic anarchy and democratic totalitarianism have been able to seize upon pieces of what is historically identifiable as an American idea of democracy. In the culturally and politically influential churches the recent attraction has been chiefly to the totalitarian side of the spectrum, particularly at those points where American influence touches the rest of the world. Thus, it is urged that if America is true to its democratic ideals, it will "get on the right side of the global revolution." When it comes to specifics, the "right side" of the revolution is almost invariably Marxist-Leninist. This understanding of America's responsibility for democracy informed influential sectors of the religiously based protest against the war in Vietnam and is today voiced with respect to "liberation movements" in Southern Africa and, more explicitly, in Central and South America.

While amenable to several interpretations, both creative and perverse, the American idea of democracy is not so plastic or vacuous that it escapes general definition. In 1980 the Institute on Religion and Democracy was established in Washington, D.C., in order to counter the totalitarian bias in some of the churches and thus to help restore the credibility of religious witness on questions of international politics. The Institute adopted "Christianity and Democracy" as its statement of philosophy and purpose, and a few passages from that statement indicate what might become an operative consensus in the religious communities about what is meant by democracy. (The fact that I agree with the statement is no doubt attributable in part to my having authored it.)

> Democratic government is limited government. It is limited in the claims it makes and in the power it seeks to exercise. Democratic government understands itself to be accountable to values and to truth which transcend any regime or party. Thus in the United States of America we declare ours to be a nation 'under God,' which means, first of all, a nation under judgment. In addition, limited government means that a clear distinction is made between the state and the society. The state is not the whole of the society, but is one important actor in the society. Other institutions—notably the family, the Church, educational, economic and cultural enterprises—are at least equally important actors in the society. They do not exist or act by sufferance of the state. Rather,

these spheres have their own peculiar sovereignty which must be respected by the state. . . . Most importantly, democratic government does not seek to control or restrict the sphere of religion in which people affirm, exercise and share their ultimate beliefs about the world and their place in it.

The statement goes on to discuss political participation, equality, human rights, and other facets of democratic governance. Its treatment of all these facets is informed by Reinhold Niebuhr's maxim: "Man's capacity for justice makes democracy possible, but man's inclination to injustice makes democracy necessary." Although the statement is very restrained in what it says about economics, that part of the statement has come under harsh attack for suggesting the possibility of a moral defense of capitalism. What the statement says is this:

As democratic government does not seek to absorb the sphere of religion, so it does seek to respect the autonomy of cultural and economic life. With respect to the last, there is much debate about the relationship between democracy and capitalism. Whatever the economic achievements of capitalism, and they are considerable, our primary concern is to preserve and strengthen democracy. We believe that the personal and institutional ownership and control of property—always as stewards of God to whom the whole creation belongs—contributes greatly to freedom. We note as a matter of historical fact that democratic governance exists only where the free market plays a large part in a society's economy.

Some more fervent proponents of capitalism have

criticized the statement for being tepid and half-hearted. Yet the leadership of the culturally formative churches in America have understandably interpreted the statement and the Institute as a frontal assault upon their position. That position conventionally includes the proposition that socialism is a necessary moral ideal and that capitalism is (and this is regularly stated in so many words) incompatible with Christian teaching. The same leadership, in its pronouncements on democracy, routinely speaks of democracy in terms of equality rather than of liberty. Indeed, the very word liberty—except as a cognate of "liberation struggle"—is deemed to be a euphemism for economic exploitation. The controversy engendered by the Institute on Religion and Democracy has been the subject of articles not only in the religious press but also in mass circulation secular magazines and on national television. The controversy shows no signs of abating, nor should it any time soon. The conventional wisdom in the culturally formative churches has been building for decades and it will likely take a decade or more for a corrective to take effect, if indeed that is possible.

By the culturally formative churches I mean those churches—notably the Methodist, Presbyterian, and Congregational Churches—which style themselves as "main-line Protestant." These churches have historically exercised the Puritan mission of giving moral and theological definition to American life. While in that particular sense they are "main-line," it should not be thought that they represent the majority of Christians in America. The main-line churches are the minority and they are in statistical decline. Some analysts suggest they are in statistical decline because they have for a long time been in spiritual decline—reflecting secular cultural assumptions rather than challenging such assumptions with truth claims that are distinctively religious or Christian.

In both numbers and vitality, majority Christianity in America is composed of Roman Catholics, Lutherans, and the variegated world of "evangelicalism" (the largest single constellation in the last category being the Southern Baptist Convention). America, it is to be remembered, is a society in which over 90 percent of the population claims to believe in God, which is about as close as survey research can come to unanimity. Close to 80 percent of the population claims to belong to a church, and the churches themselves number about 60 percent of the population on their membership rolls. On any given weekend, according to the Gallup Poll, nearly fifty percent of the population claims to have attended church or synagogue. (The Jewish population is about three percent of the whole, although, of course, a smaller percentage than that is religiously active.) Religion is by far the largest network of voluntary associations in American life. In view of the sheer size of the phenomenon, it is not surprising that there are various understandings of religion's approach to social issues, and particularly to the idea of democracy.

Until fairly recently the Protestant main line—those churches belonging to the National Council of Churches and the World Council of Churches—had unquestioned leadership in relating religion to culture, society, and politics. That leadership has been eroded as more and more of those who speak for the main line have succumbed to the "great reversal" of the traditional understanding of America's role in world history. That is, though America was once thought to be the bearer of a universal promise, it is now condemned as the carrier of the disease of imperialist capitalist oppression. It would be unfair and inaccurate to suggest that most main-line leaders would put the matter that bluntly. It is both fair and accurate, however, to say that among the bureaucrats most responsible for "church and society" issues this assumption about America's vicious influence in world history is pervasive. In addition to having dramatic consequences in the alienation of grass-roots constituency, the ideological posture of "church and society" bureaucracies has almost silenced other leaders who might be inclined to an affirmation of a more traditional understanding of America's benign influence. In a recent Roper survey done for *This World* magazine, the proposition was put: "On balance, and considering the alternatives, American influence is a force for good in the world today." Among teachers of theology and religion who responded, barely half agreed with the proposition, the rest being unsure or in disagreement. Were one to isolate those respondents teaching social ethics and moral theology, the fields relating more directly to political issues, the percentage affirming America's benign influence ("on balance and considering the alternatives") would no doubt be sharply reduced.

This loss of moral confidence in the American experiment, while characteristic of main-line leadership, is hardly characteristic of most religious leadership or of the millions of Americans who *are* the Church in the United States. It is simply that those sectors of religion which have historically provided a "moral legitimation" for the experiment are no longer doing so. (Moral legitimation, it should be emphasized, does not mean uncritical affirmation. It refers rather to that sense of purpose by which the experiment can be criticized within the context of essential affirmation.) Wilfredo Pareto, among others, reminds us that societal functions do not go unexercised just because traditional elites weary of exercising them. Pareto's notion of "the circulation of elites" is instructive in our effort to understand the role of religion in American democracy.

For a variety of reasons, the traditional main-line Protestant elite has wearied of providing a religiously grounded moral legitimation for the American idea of democracy and its defense and advance in the world. The "circulation of elites" suggests that another sector of American religion should be moving into the vacuum created. To paraphrase Spinoza, transcendence abhors a vacuum. American society is awaiting a new articulation of transcendent purpose. In many ways, this would appear to be the Roman Catholic "moment" in American history. For complicated reasons that cannot be detailed here, there is reason to believe that Roman Catholic leadership is missing that moment. There is another large sector of the American religious community, however, that is not at all shy about moving into the vacuum.

It is called the Religious New Right and is best known by the generic name of Moral Majority. It was the object of fevered and usually alarmist attention in connection with the elections of 1980. Since its appearance, many in the "liberal main line" and the secular media have declared that it is a momentary aberration in American life, a blip on the screen, as it were. Those who believe that the moral majoritarians will soon go away are, I believe, whistling in the dark. Emerging from the worlds of evangelicalism and fundamentalism, the moral majoritarians represent millions of Americans who are coming in from a 50-year exile in the wilderness.

By the 1920s, the evangelical/fundamentalist sector was drummed out of "respectable" circles of discourse in America's universities, seminaries, and communications media, most notably in the infamous "monkey trial" over the teaching of evolution in Tennessee. While in exile, they did not simply lick their wounds. Rather, they developed their own networks of education and communication and gathered millions of adherents who were looking for a faith that seemed to offer a measure of certitude in an increasingly uncertain world. After World War II they began to return, first as academically respectable "neo-evangelicals" and later as less varnished fundamentalists. What burst into public consciousness in the period immediately before the 1980 elections had been building for a very long time. For decades it had been assumed, with some justice, that these folks were politically and socially quietist, resigned to the rule of "unbelievers" in this world while they focused their attention upon the world to come. The great change now is that a substantial part of this community has gone political, making a strong bid to become the new elite in the moral legitimation of American life.

The leadership of this would-be elite is nothing if not certain about America's providential purpose in world history. It is not so clear that it understands that purpose to be the advancement of liberal democracy. The stated purpose *is* powerfully anticommunist, and thus is postured against the chief ideological adversary of liberal democracy. In its international dimensions, the stated purpose is linked to apocalyptic scenarios of "Bible prophecy" which have a most particular place for the state of Israel, including an anticipated final showdown between the U.S. and the U.S.S.R. in the expected Armageddon. Domestically, its understanding of America is tainted by strains of theocracy that some fear is not entirely sensitive to democratic freedoms essential to a pluralistic society.

While I am no prophet, my hunch is that to the extent the Religious New Right becomes the culture-defining elite or a part of that elite, it will no longer be identifiable as the Religious New Right. That means it will be tempered, domesticated, and nuanced in a manner continuous with the respect for diversity that has usually characterized American democracy.

Today, however, the Religious New Right is strident and confrontational. It understands itself as conducting a crusade against the infidels. Francis A. Schaeffer's *A Christian Manifesto* and John Whitehead's *The Second American Revolution* call, in effect, for civil war aimed at "turning America around" to be "the Christian nation" of its constituting vision. These and similar calls to arms sell in the many hundreds of thousands. It is a curiosity of considerable significance that the idea of "Christian America" is today almost the exclusive property of what is viewed as the radical right. Yet, as recently as 1931, the Supreme Court of the United States could (in *U.S.* v. *Macintosh*), without fear of contradiction, observe that America is a Christian nation. From a purely sociological view, it is self-evident that the great majority of Americans are Christians and that they consciously attribute their values to the Judeo-Christian tradition. Until the 1960s the assertion that America is in some sense a Christian nation would have been considered indisputable also in most main-line and liberal Protestant churches.

The idea that America is a "secular society" is of relatively recent vintage. The militant religionists of the New Right charge that it is an idea propagated by a small cabal of "secular humanists" who have, with the collusion of the courts, interpreted the doctrine of "separation of church and state" to mean the separation of religion from public policy. However extreme and paranoid the charges from the Religious New Right, I believe they have kicked a trip wire alerting us to some troubling changes in the general culture. As we have seen, from a sociological viewpoint American society is pervasively, if confusedly, religious. Nor can it be a matter of there being a secular *state* in a pervasively religious *society*. Such a dysjunction between state and society would be a formula for governmental delegitimation in a democratic society. And that, I believe, is precisely what we are witnessing.

Until a few years ago a more or less secure majority among social theorists agreed that there is a necessary linkage between modernization and secularization; as a society becomes more modern, so they reasoned, it would inevitably be more secular. Today in America the consensus is being reversed, with the suggestion emerging that with increased rationalization and specialization, the need for an overarching "meaning system" becomes more urgent. The orientation that is being challenged now is the orientation that has led to what I have called the naked public square. The naked public square is the situation in which public space—physical, psychological, legal—is denuded of religiously grounded values. The naked public square of secular*ism* is a very dangerous place for democracy. In this situation there are no transcendent notions of excellence nor transcendent checks upon evil. It is especially dangerous for minorities who are vulnerable to raw majoritarianism.

Of particular interest in recent years is the work of Jewish intellectuals who are challenging some of the presuppositions of "secular America." For some years it was thought in American Jewry that the more secular the society became the safer it would be for Jews and other minorities. Today it is more widely acknowledged that unless democratic rights are undergirded by religiously based values, they provide only a very feeble inhibition against the excesses of majority rule. In world-historical terms, the democratic ideal is also naked to the assaults of other belief systems, notably of Marxist-Leninist rule. It may be that among those with first-hand experience of Marxist-Leninist rule there are very few who find it a plausible belief system; however, lacking that experience, many American intellectuals and religious leaders are enamored of what Peter Berger terms an alternative "plausibility structure," an alternative way of "putting the world together." This explains in large part the excitement and sense of fresh discovery with which sundry versions of "Christian Marxism" are being embraced today.

The task today is to reestablish the linkages between Judeo-Christian religion and the democratic experiment. It is not enough that there be a general religious revival, though significant evidence suggests that such a revival is in fact underway. Unless the ideal of democratic freedom is conceptually revitalized, the energies of religious revival can be moved also into antidemocratic directions. In the constituting period of the 18th century, it was thought that democratic theory, however deistic or agnostic its formulation, would be undergirded and overarched by religious belief. There was, in Berger's phrase, a "sacred canopy" legitimating the democratic enterprise. For this reason the two "religion clauses" in our First Amendment to the Constitution were deemed so crucial. Of the two clauses, the "free exercise" clause had priority, with the "no establishment" clause being in the service of free exercise of religion. In the last several decades, however, the "no establishment" clause has often been given priority, thus bifurcating religiously based values from the public square. One consequence of this has been the collapse of what Alasdair MacIntyre defines in his *After Virtue* as a "public ethic," with the result that democratic ideals are left naked to their adversaries.

In this essay I have dwelt chiefly upon the American situation. The connections between religion and democracy in the European context are no doubt different in many respects. One can pause only to note the dramatic difference in the vitalities of institutionalized religion in Europe today. I make no apology for dwelling on the American situation, however. It is what I know best. In addition, America and its influence in the world is, for better or worse, the chief bearer of the democratic ideal today and for the foreseeable future. This is not a statement of hubris but an acknowledgement of the fact that in the absence of American example and influence, it is hard to see how the democratic proposition could be a significant agent of world-historical change.

This returns us, then, to the idea of America's moral purpose, even a kind of "destiny." The notion of "manifest destiny" is widely pilloried today. Yet destiny is but another word for purpose. The American destiny may not be manifest today. It is more likely tortuously obscured and therefore appropriately described in tones closer to those of Abraham Lincoln than to those of Theodore Roosevelt. Lincoln spoke of America as an "almost chosen" people, and he anguished over the ways in which providential purpose may be entangled with the conflicts of his day. With the same modesty, but also with the same urgency and courage, we must today reconsider the meaning of America in a global context. One theologian who is doing this with great care is Wolfhart Pannenberg of the University of Munich. He dares in *Human Nature,*

Election, and History to propose that we reconsider the meaning of "election" as a category for understanding contemporary politics among nations. If America is "elected" by God, he suggests, it is not because of any inherent moral superiority. It is rather because America has a singular opportunity, and therefore a singular responsibility, for the advancement of human freedom.

This is an audacious line of inquiry that runs counter to prevailing biases in American and Western thinking, both secular and religious. But for a people incorrigibly religious, for a nation with the soul of a church, it is a line of inquiry that must not be evaded. The alternative is an increased corrosion of confidence, an ever more severe delegitimation of the democratic experiment, with the result that the field of world-historical change will be left to ideational forces that are hostile to freedom. The corrosion may already be too far advanced. The naked public square may be so entrenched that it will successfully resist critical redirection by religiously grounded values. Even if there is a religious renascence, there is no guarantee that it will be joined to a revitalized democratic ideal. I could empower simply a resurgence of jingoistic nationalism. Or it could become yet more closely linked to ideological forces unfriendly to democratic freedom.

These are among the many uncertainties. Yet I believe ours is a moment, perhaps even a biblical *kairos*, in which we are called upon to resume Lincoln's explorations into providential purpose. America may not be the last best hope of man on earth, but for men and women who are committed to democratic freedom the future is bleak in the absence of America's example and influence. In such absence, it is just conceivable that islands of democratic freedom could be sustained in an otherwise totalitarian and authoritarian world. But the hope that humanity's future will be one of democratic freedom could not be sustained. For this reason, so much of our common future depends upon the moral and religious re-legitimation of the most democratic idea in America.

Malcolm Muggeridge has written:

> If I accept, as millions of other Western Europeans do, that America is destined to be the mainstay of freedom in this mid-twentieth century world, it does not follow that American institutions are perfect, that Americans are invariably well-behaved, or that the American way of life is flawless. It only means that in one of the most terrible conflicts in human history, I have chosen my side, as all will have to choose sooner or later, and propose to stick by the side I have chosen through thick and thin, hoping to have sufficient courage not to lose heart, sufficient sense not to allow myself to be confused or deflected from this purpose, and sufficient faith in the civilization to which I belong, and in the religion on which that civilization is based, to follow Bunyan's advice and endure the hazards and humiliations of the way because of the worth of the destination.

Is America really that critical to our common future? Yes, I suspect it is. As an American, I wish it were not so.

Rev. Neuhaus, author of *The Naked Public Square: Religion and Democracy in America* and other political and religious studies, is Director of The Rockford Institute/New York, Center on Religion and Society.

IV.

FREEDOM AND UNFREEDOM

9.

Confronting "The Russian Question": The Ideological Journey of a Generation

Melvin J. Lasky

I once had the audacity, many years ago, to put a question to Winston Churchill about the art of rhetoric, and more especially about his artful effectiveness as a parliamentarian, exhibited for so long during the stormy question-time of the House of Commons. His reply was, I suppose, very Churchillian: "Address yourself to the relevant point, if you can.... Reply directly, if you must.... But quickly, briefly, succinctly! ... And then go on, as you wish, to say what you always wanted to say." In this spirit I shall only say about the announced topic "The Obligations of Free Nations" that nations must feel obliged to think hard about the nature of freedom, its advantages and its perils, with some brilliant and refreshing realism. With that said, I want to go on, with Churchillian brashness (if not, alas, his eloquence), to consider an aspect of modern thought and ideology which ever since its dramatic statement by Tocqueville a hundred and fifty years ago has bewitched our intellectual classes. I mean the prediction that two superpowers would come to dominate the politics of the globe, and that each of these would be obliged to act as a national system in accordance with the spirit of its culture and its institutions, one in terms of political liberty and personal individuality, and the other in terms of statist coercion and collective servility.

There are, of course, many ways of telling the story of the relationship between America and Russia over the last 65 years of turbulent history, from the time of Lenin's October Revolution to the present dangers of a nuclear war between Washington and Moscow. I could offer a technical study of power-politics between two landmasses in the Eastern and Western hemispheres which have emerged as the two superpowers in the last half of the 20th century. I could also have prepared a detailed analysis of foreign policy and diplomacy, taking us through from the shock of the treaty of Brest Litovsk after World War I to the collapse of SALT II and the new shock of the invasion of Afghanistan. I prefer to tell the story another way, in a more personal manner: the story of my own generation of Americans whose lives span almost this whole historical period and whose involvement with Marxist ideas, liberal ideals, and ideological passions generally may help explain the explosive issue of communism and anticommunism in a more illuminating and truthful perspective than we normally encounter.

I say "personal," and I mean to begin with the recent invitation which I received to visit Russia for the first time. Why was a journey to Russia such a deeply moving experience for me? Even to ask such a question is to risk appearing to indulge in a perfunctory bit of sentimentalism. Of course, to be in Moscow can be said to be exciting in the conventional way that being in the land of the Pyramids or in the Temple of the Thousand Buddhas is for the tourist. I do not mean to imply this. Nor do I mean to suggest, at the other extreme of spiritual adventure, that melodramatic search for "roots" that has in our day become the new mode for establishing a deeper identity, for finding oneself and one's true sources. My sense of curiosity, of fascination, and in a way of fulfillment in being there, an American in Moscow, was neither so superficial nor so profound. I have very little talent for sightseeing, and so the extra heartbeat comes not from the first glimpse of the ancient towers of Muscovy. Nor do I bear the wounds of some crisis of uprooted identity which would painfully bleed again by standing on the ancestral land of my forefathers, by standing again on the vast Russian plain where the Kantoroviches and Chernilowskis once tried to eke out an existence, some to leave an unhappy czarist homeland to seek freedom in America, others to perish hopelessly in the gas chambers of a cruel German conqueror.

To be sure, none of us can escape history by turning away from the past which once involved us in hope and tragedy. Indeed, I can recall my very first "political memory" as a young boy growing up in New York: it was my mother's story, told in fear and trembling, of when she was a little girl growing up in then-Russian Poland, during the Cossack terror of those anti-Semitic days in Lodz after the repression of the Revolution of 1900. But the "Burden of History" which I felt myself carrying on my shoulders as an

American in Moscow was of quite a different character. It was more abstract and intellectual; it has more to do with the pains of cultural and ideological experience. It has to do with a personal education as part of a whole generation coming to maturity (as I have suggested) in an era when two great peoples and nation-states—offshoots to the East and to the West of a central European civilization—came to dominate the world political scene and to confront each other in a dramatic and dangerous duel.

This American generation of which I was a part, and whose spiritual trials and tribulations I should like to share with you, formed what is widely referred to as the New York intelligentsia and of whom it would not be immodest to say that it played a special and not unimportant role in the development of our contemporary political culture or, perhaps better put, the American intellectual temper. Over the last 40 or 50 years it produced the writers and thinkers who thrashed about in the sparkling water of ideology. Some became Marxists, and tried to refine the methods of historical materialism into a more subtle and "nonvulgar" instrument of analysis. Others became anti-Marxists and warned against the errors of a closed, dogmatic system of thought. Some were socialists who became convinced that America was different, was "exceptional," and that the United States would find its own peculiar road to progressive social development. Others were literary cosmopolitans or cultural nationalists, who believed either that America would become "European" or that it would lose its way; or they were persuaded that "only in America" could the novelist or the poet or the painter or the musical composer find a true, authentic, viable inspiration. Some read Schumpeter and John Maynard Keynes on the nature of capitalism to find new ways of reconciling the old dynamic economy with the new ideals of social democracy. Others read Oswald Spengler and Ortega y Gasset (not to mention Horkheimer, Adorno, and Marcuse, who came as refugees and settled with us in Columbia University's Morningside Heights) and became alarmed at the prospects of a violent mass society which might produce only authoritarian responses to its problems of disorder. Our curiosity and our concern for mankind (while not moving beyond the Hudson) knew no bounds. We were eclectic, argumentative, indefatigably high-minded. We confronted old questions, without reluctance accepting new and utterly different labels . . . most dramatically so when the young Marxist-Trotskyist intellectual with whom I used to have animated discussions in the "alcoves" of City College became the acknowledged leader of the Neo-Conservative movement in America (Irving Kristol). Another fellow-student in the alcove always "revising" to the right has recently summed up his disdain for the hoary categories of left and right by putting his final position thus: "I'm a socialist in economics, a liberal in politics, and a conservative in culture" (Daniel Bell).

But what I am trying to suggest to you, and I think it is important as well as surprising, is that at the heart of all this intellectual turbulence was what we called *"The Russian Question."* One of the best literary critics of this generation, Lionel Abel, once wrote in a Memoir that those were the days when New York City was a province, a *rayon*, a part of Russia! And when at one point or another in our quest to be cosmopolitan internationalists and citizens of the world we got around to reading Russian literature, to reading Dostoevski, there in *Karamazov* we found the Russian mirror image of all our American talk, the talk about what Dostoevski called "the eternal questions":

> ...talking about nothing but the eternal questions.... What do you believe, or don't you believe at all.... Of the eternal questions of the existence of God and immortality. And those who do not believe in God, talk of socialism or anarchism, of the transformation of all humanity on a new pattern. So that it all comes to the same. They're the same questions turned inside out.

What, then, was so special about "the Russian Question" that held us so disputatiously in its grip? Was it merely because so many of our grandfathers had been preoccupied in the old Russian shtetl with fine Talmudic dialectics? But then there was George F. Kennan, whose lifelong preoccupation with Russian history and politics had completely different roots: perhaps the memorable experience of his namesake and uncle, the other George Kennan, who wrote a famous book about his visits to political prisoners in Siberian camps during the czarist regime.

Could it be that "the Russian Question"—and the necessity for each of us to take "a clear position" on it—was indeed a turning inside-out of grand questions which have tormented men's minds throughout human history? Did that history have a meaning? Could a utopian dream of establishing a good society on earth ever be realized? Was revolution, rather than reform, the proper means for advancing humanitarian purposes? Would great and needed changes first take place in one country, which might be backward; or in an advanced country which had the shiny technology; or everywhere at once in a world-revolutionary overturn? Were the virtues and vices of men and women determined by historic social systems and thus changeable, malleable? The Marxist-Leninist revolution of October 1917 put these, and so many other issues, on an urgent agenda. We worked through the items on the agenda point by point.

I should really make it clear, and avoid any possible misunderstandings, that although I have been emphasizing one particular generation, one essentially confined to New York, the general analysis is not restricted to the experiences of one particular ethnic group. All of America (except, of course, for the poor native Indians, long declining on their reservations) consists of foreigners. President Franklin Roosevelt, a proud patrician of 17th-century Dutch ancestry, once outraged a meeting of the chauvinistically self-centered Daughters of the American Revolution, all presumably descendents of the earliest colonists, by beginning his address: *"Fellow immigrants."* Indeed, there have always been two souls in every American breast: one from the Old World and one from the New. A recurrent theme in the history of the "Redeemer Nation" has been its internationalism, its need to stand for universal ideals, its sense of a "world mission." From Woodrow Wilson to Henry Kissinger, whether Scottish Presbyterian or Jew from Franconian Fürth, American statecraft has always evinced ambiguities and ambivalences that have a certain doubleness in American foreign policy, with one shaping it as if he were Martin Luther or John Knox, the other as if he were Bismarck or Metternich. Old European images contribute the basic metaphors for American political language, sometimes making it profound, sometimes grotesque. Roosevelt's Secretary of State, Cordell Hull, was very impressed with Joseph Stalin ("Uncle Joe," as he called him) and thought he would have made a very fine U.S. Senator. John Reed, a witness of the October Revolution, was convinced that the "Ten Days that Shook the World" would issue in a new social order fulfilling all the ideals of the French and American Revolutions. Lincoln Steffens looked at Soviet society as if it were a practical piece of machinery and made his famous pronouncement: "I have seen the future and it works!"

Soon after President Roosevelt recognized Russia in 1933, finally giving it the formal diplomatic recognition which Woodrow Wilson had withheld from it for its betrayal of the Allied cause at the end of the First World War, the famous era of "the Fellow Travelers" began. The locomotive of history was on the move, and all liberal Americans had to travel progressively in the same direction. I can remember following, as a boy, the weekly dispatches from Moscow by Louis Fischer in *The Nation*: all singing praises to the great and good society struggling to be born. Our favorite films—"Hollywood" was only a tawdry dream factory—were shown at a little Manhattan cinema, the *Cameo* off Times Square, where we were overwhelmed by the masterpieces of Eisenstein and Pudovkin, the heroic *Chapayev*, the Maxim Gorky trilogy. Occasionally there was a sour note: I recall the sensational articles of a Russian refugee named Victor Chernavin about alleged forced-labor camps in Siberia. But these were surely not to be believed, for they had been published in the right-wing, reactionary Hearst press. But what of the growing testimony from the disenchanted left—from Leon Trotsky, from George Orwell in Spain, from John Dos Passos and John Dewey and Sidney Hook? By the time of the Hitler-Stalin pact of August 1939, sealing (as Molotov told von Ribbentrop) their "friendship in blood"—and the reference was to the double invasion of Poland—the basis for a new critical ideological attitude had emerged: a strong libertarian anti-Soviet current which was to come to high tide in the post-1945 years of the Cold War. I myself, as a young American lieutenant in the Germany of the '45 Potsdam Agreement, was almost court-martialled in Frankfurt (or rather, in our U.S. Army headquarters in nearby Hoechst) for refusing to refer to "our gallant Soviet ally" as a "freedom-loving democracy." Two years later I was almost expelled from the U.S. Occupation Zone—as General Clay later, a bit embarrassed, confessed to me—for going so far as to condemn *all* totalitarian censorship, Soviet as well as Nazi, at a German *Schriftsteller Kongress* in East Berlin. But times were changing fast, and I was only one spokesman for a new liberal antitotalitarianism which had been shaping the mind of a whole generation of American intellectuals.

It had been a restless generation, both intellectually and emotionally. Where the heart tended to try to hold fast to old sentiments, the mind forced reconsiderations in the light of new and unexpected realities. With respect to "the Russian Question," as should be abundantly clear, the opinions of this American generation were constantly in flux. But looking back now on almost fifty years of argument and debate, I am struck by the fact that certain sentiments and certain reconsiderations remained constant with us, either uppermost in our mind or anchored deep down in our hearts.

What are these principles or sentiments or attitudes? *One* would be this: that no land, no culture, no people can be contemplated through a simple pair of colored spectacles. That whether it is Russia or America or Germany (the Kaiser's, Hitler's, or Adenauer's), whether it embodies the "European spirit" or the "Slav soul"—each country presents complexities, subtleties, open and challenging questions which prevent any kind of primitive black-white or plus-minus conclusions. As Edmund Burke once said, "You cannot indict a whole nation." This is not to say at all that basic philosophical and political judgments need to be suspended forever or until all the dialectical possibilities have been exhausted. No; working hypotheses are welcome, are necessary, are illuminating. But they need always to be examined and re-examined with an honest critical spirit; new evidence needs to be looked at; and there must always be an inner readiness to admit when a thesis has to be revised and when perhaps one was—unfortunately—mistaken.

Thus, when we were young students and began to concern ourselves with more than the national-patriotic subjects which preoccupy an American schoolboy on the nature of the American Revolution of 1776 (and was it really a "Revolution" or rather a colonial war of independence? Surely the two were not the same); or the problem of the Civil War between the Southern slave states and Northern free states (and was it really "necessary" and "inevitable" that so many millions had to perish on the battlefield?)—when, as I say, we lifted our eyes up to the wide world, we found ourselves yet again trying to pick our way between old clichés and new insights, between a variety of intellectual propositions.

We started, or at least many of us did, by breaking our heads over Tocqueville. Alexis de Tocqueville then represented for us, and still to a large extent does now, the great political mind of the 19th century. Here was wisdom not only about the nature of democratic institutions, as analyzed so brilliantly in his books on *Democracy in America* (published in the 1830s); here also was wisdom about the essential gradualist nature of all sound democratic changes and, especially, about the romantic revolutionism which seized his own French society in 1848 as it has so often since, wisdom that would stand the test of time—as that of no other political analyst of the last century (and I bar not even Karl Marx here) would. What about his famous thesis on Russia? Was it true, as he wrote on the last page of the first volume of *Democracy in America* (a page that has been quoted almost as much perhaps as the phrases of Marx's pamphlets), that America—and he was writing, mind you, a hundred and fifty years ago!—represented the principle of the free Individual, and Old Russia the principle of the Mass or the unfree Collective, with the result that one would issue in republican liberties and the other in autocratic despotism?

We taught ourselves to refrain from what Tocqueville himself called "terrible over-simplification." We taught ourselves to disentangle glib literary formulations from the historical realities. So we began to read Pushkin. And in Pushkin we found a kindred spirit, one that put the lie to the idea that—as we were sometimes taught—"Slav" has an affinity with "slave." We were moved by his heartening poem for the Decembrists and their ill-fated struggle for Russian freedom, with those fine lines:

> Keep your patience proud;
> The bitter toil shall not be lost,
> The rebel thought unbowed. . . .

Yet he also gave us gentle, civilized reminders, as in his novella, *The Captain's Daughter*:

> Young man! If my notes ever fall into your hands, remember that the best and most permanent changes are those due to the softening of morals and manners and not to any violent upheavals.

In Alexander Herzen, too, we found a kindred spirit; and reading his works likewise put an end to certain received and conventional theses about how "deeply different" the course of Russian political thought had been. Condemned as it was to develop under the shadows of feudal habits, priestly obscurantism, and autocratic repression, it necessarily tended to extremes: to a moody Slavic mysticism on the one hand, or a naive revolutionary romanticism on the other. Reading Herzen we found a Russian intellectual who was neither "Western" nor "Eastern," but a liberating spirit in the great cosmopolitan and universal tradition of an inquiring mind, devoted to humane and humanist values, and always ready to review old *idées fixes*.

What a splendid moment it was for us to discover in the 19th-century Russian political literature his "Letters to an Old Comrade," written in 1869 to Mikhail Bakunin, his old friend and comrade. How provocative it was for us to find Herzen tantalizing us with a motto from Jeremy Bentham, the English reformer, on the relations between *Ends* and *Means*! How instructive it was for us, plagued by similar and related problems in a distant Euro-American context, to ponder Herzen's break with Bakunin over such fundamental questions as violence or reform, fanaticism or reasonableness, revolution or evolution. Herzen wrote: "The term 'gradual progress' holds no terror for me, discredited though it is by the vacillations and mistakes of diverse reformers. 'Gradual progress,' like continuity, is an inalienable part of every process."

Herzen defended the principle of compromise against "a headlong dash forward." He warned Bakunin against the attempt to establish "the new order, the new form of emancipation by resorting to massacre," of "liberation by means of the guillotine." Herzen tried to put his finger on the difference that had come to divide them:

> You tear along, as before, filled with passion of destruction which you take for creative passion. . . . I do not believe in the former revolutionary paths. . . . I do not believe that people who prefer destruction and brute force to evolution and amicable agreements are really serious. (*Selected Philosophical Works* [Moscow, 1956], pp. 576-95)

I confess that this is a curious *state of affairs* in the intellectual relationship between Americans and Russians. If our American tradition made us into Jeffersonians, the Russian liberal tradition made us into Herzenites. I want very much to emphasize this—it is not this or that theory or thesis of Jefferson or Herzen, this or that bit of poetry from Pushkin or Walt Whitman, that leads us to a new truth or ideology or *Weltanschauung*. Not at all; in fact, quite the contrary. I emphasize it because it seems to me (and, if I may say so, this recognition became part of the intellectual temper of my whole generation in the West), there is a realm of the spirit quite apart from, and beyond—indeed, higher than—the stiff unbending squat structures of ideology and counterideology which lie low across the terrain, like so many pillboxes of a Maginot or Siegfried line. It is the realm of the inquiring spirit, of minds that refuse to stop learning, of intellectuals who are willing to seek out other cultures, to share in their achievements and failures. We must all come out of our fixed emplaced fortresses, too crowded to let us breathe in, too close to let us think. If it was ideas, if it was books, if it was arguments about war and peace, about prosperity and progress, which originally drove us into our narrow pillboxes then it will be, again, ideas, books, and arguments which will take us out into the open fields.

I trust that I have not disguised my deep pleasure that my own American generation did not accept—at least, not for long—the clichés, the platitudinous conventions of the zeitgeist, of most of our books and newspapers on "the Russian Question." We disputed everything, and came to our own persuasions. Some of us had natural preferences and antipathies, of course. Some liked or disliked the work of, say, Maxim Gorky—but how much of a surprise was there in store for us, when we began to read a little more deeply, a little more widely and came across, for example, an edition of those unforgettable articles which Gorky wrote for his Moscow newspaper *New Life (Novaya Zhizn)* published in the historic year 1917. Some of us may have disliked the whole sensationalism of the circumstances in which Boris Pasternak's novel *Dr. Zhivago* became a world best-seller; but in reading it one was disturbingly struck by those memorable passages in which Pasternak writes, of that same revolutionary year, "the vast figure of Russia bursting into flames like a light of redemption for all the sorrows and misfortunes of mankind"—and of "that distant summer when the revolution had been a god come down to earth from heaven." Perhaps it was those poetic sentiments which persuaded Chairman Khrushchev (as he wrote in his *Memoirs*) to think that his ban on Pasternak's novel was one of his mistakes. Nothing is so pleasing to the Russian revolutionary

Confronting the Russian Question

mind as the theme of revolution and redemption, and the infatuation with light and flames. (After all, Lenin's paper was called *Iskra*, the spark.) One is also reminded of the striking passage in Yevtushenko's autobiography in which he writes, "No one in our family uttered the word 'Revolution' as if he were making a speech. It was uttered quietly, gently, a shade austerely. Revolution was the religion of our family."

I hope that these last remarks have not been misleading. I do not want to give the incorrect impression that my American generation, or the American intelligentsia by and large, was poring over Russian writing as in some spirit of *ex orient lux*. I am merely suggesting that as America came of age as a world power, and as some of us came to a measure of political maturity, we *"paid attention"* (to borrow the phrase of Arthur Miller): we paid attention to Russia, to her poets and propagandists, to her radical dissenting spirits and their counterparts, to skeptical liberals or cautious conservatives. We tried to comprehend, in their manifold spiritual complexities, Dostoevski's Grand Inquisitor and Turgenev's Bazarov. We allowed ourselves to be fascinated by Karamzin on his 18th-century travels, calling on Immanuel Kant in Königsberg and reporting on German anti-Semitism (in the year 1789!) on the occasion of a performance of Shakespeare's *Merchant of Venice* in Frankfurt on the Main. We made an effort to understand the pros and cons of the great Russian debates from Chernychevski to Plekhanov, from Belinsky to Peter Struve: all those deeply instructive controversies among all the stormy Westernizers and passionate Slavophiles, whether they were called Tolstoy or Blok, Solzhenitsyn or Sakharov. And we tried to come to some tentative apportionment of what arguments were logical, or reasonable, or accurate, or sympathetic, in the light of history.

So, if I say that America has learned from Russia I mean it as a clinical description, not as a *bien-pensant* prescription. Of course, the bromide of all international cultural exchange is that we should all learn from each other. I am not really concerned to what extent Russia, or even Europe in general, then or now, has "paid attention" to things American. Nor am I absolutely convinced that it is always necessary. I do not think of cultural exchange in terms of some kind of world budget of cultural trade, of literary imports and intellectual exports, and constantly calculating if there is a positive or negative balance of payments. I do not share the comfortable patriotic view of America as the teacher of the world. I am only trying to make the modest claim that our experience of Russia has been instructive, that the confrontation of the liberal American intelligentsia with the Bolshevik revolution, with Marxism-Leninism, with Russian cultural traditions, not to mention the totalitarian horrors of the Gulag Archipelago, has not been a simpleminded one, that it has developed in complex and interesting ways. It is true history, light years away from the superficial mindless chatter about "McCarthyite hysteria," "Cold War," "anticommunism," or "reds under the bed."

The phrase "Cold War" has fallen from use, but it cannot be avoided or evaded, for it remains the touchstone of the libertarian faith of an American generation whose idealism led its intellectuals to socialist beliefs and whose disenchantment took them into a passionate (if, at all times, impeccably democratic) anticommunism. What other choice was there for writers and scholars who still believed in "commitment" and "engagement"? One could be in favor of communism. Or one could be apolitically indifferent to it. Or one could be against it. I am afraid that exhausts the logical possibilities, and it resulted for us in an inescapable anticommunism. The *further* question then arises as to the moral, political, cultural and historical *content* of that opposition to a totalitarian system of the left which has failed to achieve either the welfare or the freedom it offered as its revolutionary ideals. One could oppose it, as so many Polish members of Solidarity do, because it denies free trade unions; or as the Pope does, because it prevents a chance for free religious life; or as Boris Pasternak did, because it censors literature and harasses independent writers. Let me go further. Hearst was against it because it represented something for him which he vaguely hated as "godless materialism"; and Oswald Spengler was against it because it embodied the evil of "mass man" degenerated by the "Slav soul." Needless to add, there was also the author of *Mein Kampf*, who fought a satanic phenomenon emanating from something he imagined to be "Judaeo-Bolshevismus."

Thus, antifascists could be—and were throughout most but not all of World War II—communists: like the Red Army they helped to win the war and despoil the peace. And there is no point denying that from time to time in the ranks of anticommunists there are unwelcome, or unsavory, forces, partisans of an Alfred Rosenberg fanaticism or an Ayatollah Khomeini dogmatism or a Somoza tyranny.

In other words, one can oppose a political and historic evil haphazardly or coherently, delusively or realistically, with conventional and ambiguous prejudices or informed and critical standards, in the name of an ideal good and its pragmatic benefits or on behalf of an alternative evil and its slightly revised miseries. For one must recognize that anticommunism, not unlike antinazism, is fed from the same wide variety of human motivations, embracing political, economic, cultural, moral and religious values, as well as a dark conglomeration of antipathies for something strange, foreign, and alien, something almost indefinably hateful. Simple labels like "anticommunist" or "antifascist" are often necessary in the conflict of historical forces, even if they do not by themselves clarify what it is one is opposing, or what it is one is proposing.

But I would argue and insist, without engaging in burdensome metaphysics, that the true negation of an evil is the positing of an implicit good. A consistent antitotalitarianism implies a constitution of liberty. That is the badge of honor of the devotees of freedom and the defenders of free peoples and nations.

In this light, let me look back on those 35 postwar years. I am tempted to divide that whole historic period from the old ruins of Hitler's *Reichshauptstadt* in 1945 to the new anxieties of the present day into two fundamentally, tragically different periods. I lived through both periods in Europe, as an American in Berlin, Paris, and London.

The first period—the late 1940s, the '50s, and the early '60s—is still, I think, not sufficiently appreciated as one of the great periods of European history and Western civilization: the magnificent recovery of the Old World, aided by the New World, out of the rubble of the most fratricidal war in the annals of mankind. There were moments when it was hard to believe that men and women could learn to hope again, could feel it was worthwhile to reconstruct, could find new ways of living together in a Western form of cooperation, reasonableness, and toleration which so much of our own past had murderously denied. For many of us it was symbolized by the phrase of the unforgettable *Berliner Oberburgermeister* Ernst Reuter: "the Miracle of Berlin" (*"das Wunder Berlins"*). And by that he meant that a city and a population that had been battered, corrupted and humiliated by the catastrophe of the Third Reich still was able to find enough inner resources to hold out against the Soviet Blockade in 1948-49, despite all the seductive offers of peace with coal and extra rations. In other words, anticommunism in a most surprising and heartening way won—despite the handicap of yesterday's Goebbelsian propaganda against *"der Russe als Untermensch"*—its new democratic, libertarian credentials. By the way, I should mention in passing here that I participated in a small West Berlin group, including Mayor Reuter and the young Willy Brandt, to make sure that the old phraseology (like *"der Russe"*) was never used; that there was always a distinction made between the peoples of the U.S.S.R., who were themselves oppressed, and the Soviet regime; that, in other words, the opposition to communism involved—and must be seen to involve—not race, nationalism, and pseudo-*Volkerpsychologie*, but a devotion to the real liberties of an open and free society.

This new resistance movement represented, at its profoundest political and cultural level, an astonishing self-confidence of democratic society in the West—imperfect but changing, growing, improving—in the face of a new totalitarian challenge. It resisted and rejected the threat and blandishments of Marshal Stalin and Chairman Khrushchev; it united in alliances and agreements to create military security and economic prosperity; it defended and indeed expanded intellectual liberties and cultural diversity. All (or almost all) worked together in mutual tolerance and respect—conservatives, liberals and socialists alike. Apart from the totalitarian forces, old and new—fascist or Nazi right and communist left—there was a general consensus. A free and vital liberal civilization, stretching westward from the Brandenburg Tor for some ten thousand miles, was—for all its faults, shortcomings, and evils—worthy of our support. We were proud, optimistic, self-confident, and fairly united. Out of the Cold War came a European renaissance.

In the second period I have referred to, the very word "consensus" became a dirty word. One of the classic totalitarian philosophies made a surprising comeback, as young persons in universities and young nationalist movements in the Third World turned to the illiberal principles of Marxist revolution. The once-effective union of democratic forces in the West began to disintegrate. Men on the left began to see the "seeds of fascism" in every conservative; conservatives began to detect totalitarian tendencies in every socialist; and as for the men in the center, they began to lose confidence in the middle way, the way of moderation, gradual change, and a decent respect for a mixed and various way of reconstructing social institutions. We have become afflicted with a plague of mutual recrimination. In the famous lines of the Irish poet William Butler Yeats:

> Things fall apart; the centre cannot hold . . .
> . . . anarchy is loosed upon the world . . .
> The best lack all conviction, while the worst
> Are full of passionate intensity.

In the more recent arguments framed by Aleksandr Solzhenitsyn (during his Swiss and now his

American exile), the West has been overcome by a sudden strange blindness, or at least astigmatism. It no longer recognizes the total, monstrous evil of the Gulag Archipelago. It flounders in its own social and economic problems, confused and unnecessarily conscience-stricken. It no longer knows how to answer the slogans of a new ideology of race, violence, terror, dictatorship, especially when the slogans are accompanied by promises of a peaceful togetherness reconciling the lamb and the lion. One knows the anxieties of war and peace today, but of what value is a half-century's anguished thought on "the Russian Question" when all the lessons of the past are so easily overlooked by another generation? As Saul Bellow has said, "A great deal of intelligence can be invested in ignorance when the need for illusion is deep."

I cannot hope to answer in brief the question of *why* in the last thirty-five post-War years we have witnessed a time of hope and a time of despair, a time of construction and a time of confusion, a time of certainties and a time of doubt. But in the context of my main theme—the experience of an American generation with the intellectual problem of ideology—I feel it is important to emphasize in conclusion the one special factor to which I have paid perhaps inordinate attention: the matter of intellectual style.

I have never stopped wondering over all these decades why it is so difficult for a Western intellectual to recognize both the virtues and the vices of the European-American pattern of society in which he lives, to think through its problems and processes and thus reach positions from which he can both defend our culture and criticize its faults, preserve the tradition and create it anew. He need not be wedded to any narrow national shibboleths or vested interests. He can defend prosperity and criticize its materialism. He can stand up for his own personal liberty and still desperately want its extension to the oppressed and enslaved. He can believe in the achievement of what is called Atlantic Civilization and know that no man is an island unto himself and no culture an ocean to itself—there are always before us the Indian Ocean and the Yellow Sea as symbols of larger engagement. Alas, this is too rarely the case. Western intellectuals are often either defensive or defeatist. The one sees only virtues to be proud of; the other detects only vices to be ashamed of. The one tends to be too complacent, the other too alienated.

Perhaps we have come to this, at the end of one American's intellectual journey: we need to be reminded of the old aphorism: The trouble with man is two-fold. . . . He cannot learn truths which are too complicated. He forgets truths which are too simple.

Mr. Lasky, author of *Utopia and Revolution* and other works, is coeditor of *Encounter* in London and editorial director of the Library Press in New York.

Onomastic Index

Abel, Lionel, 137
Adenauer, Conrad, 141
Adorno, Theodor, 137
Aristotle, 10, 12, 26, 99
Arnold, Matthew, 86

Bakunin, Mikhail, 106, 144-45
Bechet, Sidney, 6
Belinsky, Vissarion, 147
Bell, Daniel, 137
Bellow, Saul, 153
Bismark, Otto von, 139
Bochenski, Innocentius M., 7
Brandt, Willy, 151
Bunyan, John, 130
Burke, Edmund, 79-80, 90, 142

Carter, Jimmy, 115
Chalmers, Gordon, 88-89
Chernavin, Victor, 140
Chernyshevski, Nikolai, 147
Chesterton, G. K., 113
Churchill, Winston, 133
Clay, Lucius, 141
Conant, James B., 83
Cooper, Gary, 4

Dante Alighieri, 100
Dewey, John, 140
Dies, Martin, 103
Disney, Walt, 4
Dos Passos, John, 140
Dostoevski, Fedor, 137-38, 147

Eisenstein, Sergei, 140
Ewen, Stuart, 101n

Fassbinder, Rainer, 106
Fischer, Louis, 140

Fitzgerald, Ella, 5
Freud, Sigmund, 108
Friedman, Milton, 41

Galbraith, John K., 100
Goebbels, Joseph, 151
Gorky, Maxim, 140, 146
Grenier, Richard, 105-06
Gresham, Thomas, 107
Guizot, Francois, 86

Haig, Alexander, 9
Hamilton, Alexander, 117
Hardy, Thomas, 97
Hayek, Friedrich, 64
Hegel, G. W. F., 8
Hemingway, Ernest, 4
Hearst, William R., 140, 149
Herzen, Alexander, 144-45
Hitler, Adolf, 140, 141, 149, 150
Hobbes, Thomas, 22, 51
Hollander, Paul, 106
Homer, 52
Hook, Sidney, 140
Horkheimer, Max, 137
Hull, Cordell, 139
Hunt, Nelson B. and W. Herbert, (brothers), 45
Hutchins, Maynard, 83

Jay, John, 117
Jefferson, Thomas, 145
Jenner, William, 103
Jesus Christ, 9
Johnson, Lyndon, 56
Johnson, Samuel, 103

Kant, Immanuel, 147
Karamazin, Nikolai, 147

Onomastic Index

Kennan, George, 138
Keynes, John M., 136
Khomeini, Ruhollah, 149
Khrushchev, Nikita, 146, 151
Kissinger, Henry, 139
Knox, John, 139
Kristol, Irving, 96-97, 137

Laing, R. D., 102
Lasch, Christopher, 106-07
Lenin, Vladimir, 32, 42, 106, 117, 127, 134, 139, 147, 148
Lewis, C. S., 25
Lincoln, Abraham, 115, 128
Luther, Martin, 139

Madison, James, 117
McCarthy, Joseph, 103, 148
MacIntyre, Alasdair, 128
Mailer, Norman, 105
Marcuse, Herbert, 98-101, 137
Marx, Karl, 11, 17, 32, 42, 49, 97, 107, 117, 127, 134, 136, 139, 143, 148, 152
May, Rollo, 102-04
Metternich, Klemens von, 139
Miller, Arthur, 147
Milton, John, 100
Minogue, Kenneth, 108
Molotov, Vyacheslav, 140
Morgenthau, Hans, 113
Muggeridge, Malcolm, 130

Nader, Ralph, 73-74
Neilson, William A., 88
Nestor, 52
Niebuhr, Reinhold, 119
Nixon, Richard M., 67

Ortega y Gasset, José, 137
Orwell, George, 140

Pannenberg, Wolfhart, 128-29
Pareto, Wilfredo, 122-23
Pasternak, Boris, 146, 149
Plato, 10, 12

Plekhanov, Georgi, 147
Pound, Ezra, 80-81
Pudovkin, Vsevolod, 140
Pusey, Nathan, 84
Pushkin, Aleksander, 143-44

Reagan, Ronald, 41, 115
Reuter, Ernst, 151
Ribbentrop, Joachim von, 140
Robespierre, Maximilien, 106
Roosevelt, Franklin D., 56, 115, 139, 140
Roosevelt, Theodore, 128
Rosenberg, Alfred, 149

Schaeffer, Francis A., 125
Schumpeter, Joseph, 96, 136
Shakespeare, William, 100, 111, 147
Sloan, Douglas, 82, 85
Smith, Adam, 62
Solzhenitsyn, Aleksandr, 23, 30, 152-53
Somoza, Anastasio, 149
Spengler, Oswald, 137, 149
Spinoza, Baruch, 123
Stalin, Joseph, 50-51, 139-40, 151
Steinbrenner, George, 68
Struve, Peter, 147
Sukarno, 42

Thatcher, Margaret, 41
Tocqueville, Alexis Charles de, 18, 98-99, 107, 134, 142-43
Trilling, Lionel, 102
Trotsky, Leon, 137, 140
Turgenev, Ivan, 147

Voltaire (Francois Marie Arouet), 3-4

Waller, Fats, 4-5
Whitehead, John, 125
Whitman, Walt, 145
Wilson, Woodrow, 83, 115, 139

Yeats, William Butler, 152

Topical Index

academic freedom, 81, 84
advertising, 95, 100, 101, 107, 110
Afghanistan, 134
Africa, 39, 50, 118
After Virtue (MacIntyre), 128
"Ain't Misbehavin'" (Waller), 4-5
Alaska, 53
America:
   decline of, 88, 96, 153
   and democracy, 14-15, 18, 97-99,
      116-19, 124-25, 129-30, 148
   economic system of, 43-44,
      46-47, 52, 53-56
   and education, 81-86, 92
   and freedom, 3-4, 97-99, 102-03
   identity of, 112-16
   influence of, 3-4, 5-7, 112-114,
      116, 117-18, 128, 129-30, 134,
      139, 150-151, 153
   religion in, 113, 116-30, 137-38
   and Russia, 134-49, 151
American Enterprise Institute, 47
"American exception, the" 113, 136
American Revolution, 140, 142
American Sociologist, 106
Amsterdam, 52
Amtrak, 47
Les Annales de L'Education, 86
Antioch, 52
anti-Semitism, 42, 136, 147, 149
antitrust legislation, 47
Antwerp, 52
Aquilaea, 52
As You Like It (Shakespeare), 111
Athens, 12, 14, 52
Atlantic Civilization, 154
Australia, 43, 53
Austria-Hungary, 50

Berlin, 49, 141, 150, 151

Bible, 9, 57, 124
Bolshevik revolution. *See* Russian
   Revolution
bourgeoisie, 42, 96-97, 114
Brandenburg, 152
Brest Litovsk, 134
Britain, 23, 46-47, 50, 61-62, 71,
   86, 113, 115, 117
British Rail, 47
Bronx, The, 68
Brothers Karamazov, The
   (Dostoevski), 137-38, 147
Buenos Aires, 50
Byzantium, 52

California, 53
Canada, 43
capitalism, 32, 41-44, 46-47, 49-50,
   53, 55, 59-60, 62-63, 69-73,
   96-97, 100, 106, 118-19, 121,
   136-37
Capitalism, Socialism and Democracy
   (Schumpeter), 96
Captain's Daughter, The (Pushkin),
   143-44
Captains of Consciousness (Ewen),
   111n
Carnegie Endowment, 75
Catholic Church. *See* Roman
   Catholic Church
censorship, 30, 44-45, 105, 141
Chapayev (Furmanov), 140
Chicago, 50
China, 50, 54, 105
Christianity, 9, 12-13, 51, 115,
   117-18, 120-27
"Christianity and Democracy"
   (Neuhaus), 118-19
Christian Manifesto, A (Schaeffer),
   125

157

"circulation of elites," 123
citizenship training, 90-92
City of Man, The (Wagar), 88
Civil Aeronautics Board, 67
civilized norms, 87-88
Civilization and Its Discontents (Freud), 108
Civil War (American), 142
Cleveland, 50
Cold War, 141, 148-49, 152
collectivism, 39, 50, 64-66, 74-75, 134, 143
Columbia University, 137
Commentary, 105-06
Common Market. *See* European Economic Community
communism, 10, 22, 27, 32, 39, 42-43, 45, 88-89, 105-06, 124, 134, 148-49, 151
Congregational Church, 120
conservatism, 115, 137, 140, 147, 151
Constitution (American), 62, 127
consumerism, 73-74
contemporary culture, 95-97, 100-05
counseling, 101-02
Cuba, 23, 105-06

Daughters of the American Revolution, 116, 139
democracy:
   and America, 14-15, 18, 98-99, 112-13, 116-19, 124-25, 127, 129-30, 148-49
   and aristocracy, 12-14
   and communism, 124, 149-51
   definitions of, 14-17
   and economics, 48-49, 96, 119, 137
   and equality, 11-16, 19-22, 120
   and religion, 118-30
   strengths and weaknesses of, 11-13, 17-18, 97-99, 109, 151-53
Democracy in America (Tocqueville), 98, 143

Detroit, 50
Djakarta, 42-43
Dr. Zhivago (Pasternak), 146

Economic Thought and Social Change (Stanfield), 111n
education, 81-86, 89-90, 92-94, 101-02
energy, 48
England. *See* Britain
equality, 11-16, 19-22, 97-99, 110, 117, 120
"ethical ignorance," 89
Europe, 45, 50-51, 53, 113, 128, 136, 139, 141-42, 150
European Economic Community, 53
evangelicalism, 121, 123-24. *See also* Religious New Right

"failure of nerve," 110
fascism. *See* Nazism
Fathers and Sons (Turgenev), 147
Federal Communications Commission, 46-47
Federalist Papers, The, 117
fellow travelers, 140
Florence, 52
Ford Foundation, 75
Founding Fathers, 115, 117
France, 15, 53, 86, 115, 117, 140, 143
Frankfurt, 3-4, 141, 147
freedom:
   and authority, 5
   definitions, 5-6, 11-13, 17-19, 28-34, 39-41, 49-50, 79, 110
   and economics, 41, 43-47, 53, 60-61, 64-65, 74-75, 96, 119
   and equality, 19-20, 96, 113, 120
   and morality, 9-11, 30, 58, 93-94
   and peace, 9-10, 94
   and personal content, 51, 105-06, 107, 109-110
   and religion, 119-20, 124-27, 129
   and security, 20-21, 30, 96
   See also democracy and liberty

Topical Index

free market, 41-47, 50, 59-60, 70-71, 72-73, 96, 119
French Revolution, 140
fundamentalism. *See* Religious New Right

Gallup Poll, 121
General Motors, 74
Genoa, 52, 61
Germany, 17, 50, 53, 115, 141, 142, 147, 151, 152
government regulation, 44-46, 48, 55-58, 59-67, 70-71
Great Society, 56
Greece, 24, 41, 52
Gulag Archipelago, The (Solzhenitsyn), 23, 148, 153

happiness, 97-100, 105, 107
Harvard University, 83, 84
Hastings Center, 82
Higher Therapy, 101, 109
history, nature of, 7-9, 31-33, 135-36, 138-39
Hitler-Stalin pact, 140-41
Holland. *See* Netherlands
Hollywood, 140
Hong Kong, 53-54, 57
Human Nature, Election, and History (Pannenberg), 128-29

Illinois, 3
Independent Broadcasting Authority (British), 46-47
India, 50
Indians (American), 139
Indonesia, 42-43
Industrial Revolution, 41, 56
Institute on Religion and Democracy, 118, 120
intellectuals, 23, 81, 88, 134, 136-49, 152-54
Interstate Commerce Commission, 67
Ireland, 50
Iskra (*The Spark*), 147

Israel (ancient), 113
Israel (modern), 124

Japan, 53
jazz, 4-6
Judaism, 5, 42, 121, 125, 126, 138, 139
justice, 20, 91

Kenyon College, 88
Königsberg (Kalingrad), 147
Korea, 53

Latin America, 50, 117-118
Law, Legislation and Liberty (Hayek), 64
lawfulness, 67-68, 90
"Letters to an Old Comrade" (Herzen), 144-45
"Letter to the Sheriffs of the City of Bristol" (Burke), 79-80, 90
Leviathan (Hobbes), 22, 51
liberalism, 11, 88-89, 103, 108, 115, 134, 140, 145, 148, 152
liberty, 5, 79, 120, 150. *See also* freedom
libertarianism, 117, 141, 148-49, 151
London, 47, 52, 62, 150
Lutheran Church, 121

McGuffey Readers, 82
"manifest destiny," 128
Marshall Plan, 52
Marxism, 11, 17, 32, 42, 49, 97-98, 107, 117, 127, 134, 136, 139, 143, 148, 152
Mein Kampf (Hitler), 149
mental health, 101-106
mercantilism, 61-62
Merchant of Venice (Shakespeare), 147
Methodist Church, 120
Middle Ages, 24, 52
mixed economy, 65-66
Moral Majority. *See* Religious New Right

moral relativism, 83-84, 89
Moscow, 134-35, 146
Mycenae, 52

"naked public square, the," 125-26, 129
Nation, The, 140
National Council of Churches, 121
Nazism, 23, 88, 135, 151, 152
neoconservatism. *See* conservatism
Netherlands, 46, 61-62
New Deal, 56
New England, 62, 86
New Left, 96-97
New Life (Novoya Zhizn), 146
New York City, 47, 50, 52, 135-39
New York Yankees, 68
Nicomachean Ethics (Aristotle), 26
nuclear freeze, 91

oil companies, 71
One-Dimensional Man (Marcuse), 99
Oslo, 5
Oxford University, 86

Paris, 150
Parliament, 62, 133
patriotism, 85-86, 103
Peloponnesian War, 12
philanthropy, 68-69
Physical Fallacy, 42
Pisa, 52
Pisan Cantos (Pound), 80
Poland, 45-50, 140, 149
Politeia (Plato), 12
Politics (Aristotle), 99
pornography, 30, 67, 96-97
Potsdam Agreement, 141
Presbyterian Church, 120, 139
Princeton University, 83
Protestant churches, 120, 125
profit motive, 69-72
protectionism, 70-71
psychiatry. *See* mental health

Pylos, 52

radicalism, 81, 96, 100
rationing, 40
Republic and The Person, The, (Chalmers), 88-89
regional policy, 56-57
religion, 34, 108, 110, 113, 137-38. *See also* Christianity, Judaism, and Religious New Right
Religious New Right, 123-26
research, emphasis in education, 84-85, 93
Right-to-Work legislation, 55
Robinson Crusoe (Defoe), 28
Rockefeller Foundation, 75
Rockford Institute, The, 3
Roman Catholic Church, 17, 121, 123, 149
Roper survey, 122
Russia, 23, 39-40, 43, 50-51, 105, 109, 134-49, 152-53
Russian Revolution, 134, 139, 140, 146-47

Sao Paulo, 50
Saturday Review, 80-81
science, 35-36, 83, 89
Scotland, 62
Second American Revolution, The, (Whitehead), 125
secularism, 125-26
7-11 convenience stores, 107
Siberia, 138, 140
Sincerity and Authenticity (Trilling), 111n
Singapore, 53
"Slav soul," 142, 149
socialism, 22, 32, 40, 42, 120, 137, 148, 152. *See also* collectivism
Solidarity, 149
Southern Baptist Convention. *See* evangelicalism
sovereignty, 31-32
Soviet Union. *See* Russia
Spain, 115, 140

Topical Index

Sparta, 52
state monopolies, 45-47
Stoics, 12-13
subsidies, 47-48
Supreme Court (American), 125
System, das, 106

Taiwan, 53
taxation, 29, 72
"Teaching of Ethics in the Undergraduate Curriculum 1876-1976, The" (Sloan), 82, 85
television, 46-47, 49, 95-97, 108, 120
Texas, 55
Thebes, 52
This World, 122
"A Tisket, a Tasket," 5
totalitarianism, 31-33, 50-51, 63-65, 87, 105, 117-18, 141, 148-49, 151, 152
Troy, 52
Two Cheers for Capitalism (Kristol), 105n

U.S.S.R. *See* Russia
U.S. *See* America
United States Congress, 91
United States Library of Congress, 80
U.S. v. *Macintosh,* 125
University of Chicago, 83
University of Munich, 128

Venice, 52, 61
Vietnam, 105, 118
Vilna (Lithuania), 4
Virginia, 62

Washington, D.C., 118, 134
Wealth of Nations, The, (Smith), 62
welfare state, 20-22, 30, 63-64
White-Anglo-Saxon-Protestant hegemony, 115
Wirtshaftwunder, 53
World Council of Churches, 121
World War I, 113, 134, 140
World War II, 52, 83, 112-13, 124, 149, 150

Devin-Adair, Publishers, is America's foremost publisher of quality conservative books. Founded in 1911, the company has championed the cause of the thinking right and historically has published the work of major conservative writers. In recent years, Devin-Adair has increased its emphasis in this area and today is considered the leading publishing firm of the right.

The firm also has a long-standing reputation for works of significance in the fields of ecology, Irish literature, health and nutrition. It publishes superbly illustrated nature and travel books on the Eastern seaboard through its Chatham Press subsidiary.

Devin-Adair's newest emphasis is in the area of books, software and programs relating to the personal computer.

Devin-Adair operates the Veritas Book Club for conservative readers, the Ecological Book Club for nature and health audiences, and the Irish-American Book Society.

Devin-Adair, Publishers
6 North Water Street
Greenwich, Connecticut 06830

EXCELLENCE, SINCE 1911